The
Rosary

The Rosary

PRAYER COMES ROUND

I pray—for fashion's word is out
And prayer comes round again—
That I may seem, though I die old,
A foolish, passionate man.

—W. B. YEATS

GARRY WILLS

VIKING

VIKING
Published by the Penguin Group
Penguin Group (USA) Inc., 375 Hudson Street,
New York, New York 10014, U.S.A.
Penguin Group (Canada), 90 Eglinton Avenue East, Suite 700, Toronto,
Ontario, Canada M4P 2Y3 (a division of Pearson Penguin Canada Inc.)
Penguin Books Ltd, 80 Strand, London WC2R 0RL, England
Penguin Ireland, 25 St. Stephen's Green, Dublin 2, Ireland
(a division of Penguin Books Ltd)
Penguin Books Australia Ltd, 250 Camberwell Road, Camberwell,
Victoria 3124, Australia (a division of Pearson Australia Group Pty Ltd)
Penguin Books India Pvt Ltd, 11 Community Centre,
Panchsheel Park, New Delhi–110 017, India
Penguin Group (NZ), Cnr Airborne and Rosedale Roads, Albany,
Auckland 1310, New Zealand (a division of Pearson New Zealand Ltd)
Penguin Books (South Africa) (Pty) Ltd, 24 Sturdee Avenue,
Rosebank, Johannesburg 2196, South Africa

Penguin Books Ltd, Registered Offices: 80 Strand, London WC2R 0RL, England

First published in 2005 by Viking Penguin, a member of Penguin Group (USA) Inc.

1 3 5 7 9 10 8 6 4 2

Copyright © Garry Wills, 2005
All rights reserved

Grateful acknowledgment is made for permission to reprint an excerpt from "A
Prayer for Old Age" from *The Collected Works of W. B. Yeats, Volume I: The Poems,
revised,* edited by Richard J. Finneran. Copyright © 1934 by The Macmillan
Company, copyright renewed © 1962 by Bertha Georgie Yeats. Reprinted with permission of Scribner, an imprint of Simon & Schuster Adult Publishing Group.

Artwork credits appear on page 190.

library of congress cataloging in publication data
Wills, Garry,———
The Rosary: prayer comes round / Garry Wills.
p. cm.
Includes bibliographical references.
ISBN 0-670-03449-5
1. Rosary. 2. Prayer—Catholic Church. 3. Meditation—Catholic Church. I. Title
BX2163.W54 2005
242'.74—dc22   2005042283

Printed in the United States of America
Set in Janson Text   Designed by Francesca Belanger
Rosary illustration by Alexis Seabrook

To Dick Cusack

master of the revels

All translations, except from the Hebrew, are by the author. Passages in Hebrew come from the New English Bible.

Acknowledgments

For securing rights to the Tintoretto illustrations, I thank John C. Wills, of Feldman Associates. I feel special gratitude to my editor Carolyn Carlson and my agent Andrew Wylie. For keeping faith alive in a dark time I turn to the Sheil Catholic Center and to my fellows there, Dick and Nancy Cusack.

Contents

Contents

IV. THE SORROWFUL MYSTERIES

V. THE GLORIOUS MYSTERIES

Introduction

TIMELY AND TIMELESS

FOR CATHOLICS who grew up before the Second Vatican Council, saying the rosary, privately or with others, was a regular part of our lives. But in recent years the rosary has come to be stigmatized, precisely, as "preconciliar"—as theologically retrograde, a bit of folk Catholicism, a thing to be dismissed. I think that is not only regrettable but surprising. In one way the rosary is both very timely and also timeless. Timely, because meditation is something many people feel a need for today, and the rosary has long filled that need. In bookstores we find volume after volume that tells us how to seek inner peace by contemplation, by regular time-outs from the press of worldly concerns, by exercises that collect oneself within oneself, that lift one's spirit toward a higher plane of consciousness. According to Pope John Paul II, the rosary has long answered this need for contemplation:

> The West is now experiencing a renewed demand for meditation, which at times leads to a keen interest in aspects of other religions. . . . Much in vogue among these approaches are methods aimed at attaining a high level of spiritual concentration by using techniques of a psychological, repetitive,

and symbolic character. The rosary is situated within this broad gamut of religious phenomena. (28)[1]

The rosary is timely because people increasingly long for quiet and regeneration.

A discovery of the importance of silence is one of the secrets of practicing contemplation and meditation. One drawback of a society dominated by technology and the mass media is the fact that silence becomes increasingly difficult to achieve. Just as moments of silence are recommended in the liturgy, so too in the recitation of the rosary it is fitting to pause briefly after listening to the word of God, while the mind focuses on the content of a particular mystery. (31)

But the rosary is also timeless—it uses an ancient and wide-spread aid to contemplation, the rhythmic repetition of prayers said on a string of beads (the very word "bead" comes from the old Anglo-Saxon term for prayer, *bede*). This practice is found in Hindu, Buddhist, and Islamic prayer life, as well as in Christian history. The objection sometimes made to the rosary, that it is a mechanical exercise, misses the point of such bead disciplines. Changing the rhythm of one's life, freeing the mind to move in a different way, involves slowing down the tempo of thought, entering a stalled state. That is why religious ceremony of almost every kind involves incantatory, repetitious, stylized actions.

It is true that the rosary as it was said in the past could

1. John Paul II, *The Rosary of the Virgin Mary*, Apostolic Letter, October 16, 2002. All quotations from John Paul come from this apostolic letter, with the cited paragraph number.

work against contemplative patterns—when it was rattled off as a formula to be got over, was recited "to get the indulgence," or performed with others as a communal duty. But that was a distortion of the practice, which left its essence untouched. It is a form of prayer in which repetitions should be breathed in a relaxed state, as Saint Ignatius recommended. Pope Paul VI said, "By its nature the recitation of the rosary calls for a quiet rhythm and a lingering pace." (47)[2]

The rosary is more complexly articulated than some forms of bead praying. It involves the saying of four prayers in a certain combination—creed, Our Father, Hail Mary, doxology ("Glory be . . .")—and this combination can be orchestrated, as it were, in four different ways, reflecting four sets of subjects for contemplation (four sequences of gospel *mysteries*), each mystery dwelt on while one repeats the Hail Mary on each of ten beads (a *decade*). If this sounds complex in a printed description, it is very easy in practice—after all, Catholics of my generation learned to do it early in grade school.

The mysteries—the subjects of contemplation that one moves through as one says each subdivision of beads—are related aspects of Christ's life: five glad events, five sad events, five teaching events, and five glorious events. Catholics have sometimes (and sometimes rightly) been said to neglect the Bible. But contemplating the New Testament episodes while saying the rosary is a way of remedying that situation. Our meditations are meant to be not merely an escape from self, but an entry into the life of Christ. We Christians believe that we are incorporated into the risen life of Jesus, as members of

2. Paul VI, *Marian Devotion*, Apostolic Exhortation, February 2, 1974. All quotations from Paul VI are from this exhortation, with the cited paragraph number.

his mystical body. The Spirit prays in us, through Christ, to the Father. Saint Paul says, "My life is no longer mine, but Christ's in me" (Galatians 2.20). And Colossians 3.3 says, "Secretly you live with Christ in God." The rosary invites us to retire into that secret of our deeper life in Christ, to reflect on his actions and their private meaning for us, and to do this at our own pace, seeking our own peace.

An objection naturally poses itself: If our meditations are on the life of Christ, why is the most repeated prayer in the rosary said to the Virgin Mary? The Hail Mary, as used while contemplating the life of Christ, is properly a prayer for assistance in understanding that life. Pope John Paul again: "Although the repeated Hail Mary is addressed directly to Mary, it is to Jesus that the act of love is ultimately directed, with her and through her" (26). Mary is a perfect model for this, since the gospel presents her as mystified by her own son, trying patiently to probe the meaning of his actions.

—When the angel Gabriel greets her as "Highly Favored," she is stunned (*dietarachthē*) and tries to puzzle out (*dielogizeto*) what it can mean (Luke 1.29).

—After the wondrous events surrounding Christ's birth, it is said: "She kept these things for inner scrutiny *[synetērei]*, sifting them *[symballousa]* in her heart" (Luke 2.19).

—At the presentation of Jesus in the temple, when Simeon prophesies the mission of Jesus, Mary and Joseph "were astounded *[thaumazontes]* at what was being said about him" (Luke 2.33).

—Mary is not only surprised but hurt when the boy Jesus goes off for five days without telling her. She and Joseph are "dumbfounded" *(exeplagēsan)*, and she expresses her disappointment: "How, my son, could you treat us this way?" (Luke

2.48). When Jesus says he has a duty to a higher Father, Mary and Joseph "did not understand *[synēkan]* what he told them" (Luke 2.50)—but "his mother kept all he said for close scrutiny *[dietērei]* in her heart" (Luke 2.51). Father Raymond Brown notes that the verb for "observe" *(tērein)* used in 2.19 and 2.51 means "to keep a close or wary watch on."

—At the wedding in Cana, Jesus apparently rejects Mary's request that he help the people who have run out of wine: "Woman, why is your worry mine?—My time is not yet come." She does not know what he means. All she can say to the servants is: "Whatever thing he tells you, do that" (John 2.5).

—When Jesus refuses to receive Mary when she is asking for access to him, he says: "Who is my mother, who my brothers?" And looking over those seated all about him, he says, "Here is my mother, here my brothers. Whoever does what God wants, that is my brother, and sister, and mother" (Mark 3.31–35).

—When a woman cries out to Jesus, "Blessed the womb that bore you," he corrects her: "Blessed, rather, those who, hearing God's word, are its champions *[phylassontes]*" (Luke 11.27–28).

Jesus of the gospels was a continual affront even to his closest followers. Chesterton said that Christ moved about as in some higher weather system, breaking out in wraths and mercies contrary to the lower atmospherics. It could not have been easy being the mother of a walking spiritual thunderstorm. Mary had to make her way through the layers of this divine conundrum to its inmost meaning by the deepest kind of faith. We pray with her for the understanding she achieved by strenuous effort. She went before us in this quest. To ask her aid as we make the same journey is not to succumb to "Mariolatry."

It is to rely on our fellow member of the mystical body of Christ. We rely on all the other members, our brothers and sisters, to aid us. Why not turn to the greatest of the seekers, the person closest to the head of our body? If we are members of that body, so is she—we have Saint Augustine's warrant for it (Sermon Denis 25): "Mary is part of the church, a holy member, an outstanding member, a supereminent member, but a member of the whole body nonetheless."

Devotion to Mary does not divert us from the path to Christ. In fact, her very title in the Hail Mary, Mother of God (*Theotokos*), was hammered out in the debates on the nature of Christ at the Council of Ephesus. Arians there wanted to deny her that title as a way of denying the divinity of her son. They would call her only Mother of Christ (*Christotokos*). The rosary is not an exercise in superstition, but has a solid scriptural and theological grounding—a grounding in Christ. In order to emphasize this, I shall quote at the beginning of each mystery the gospel passage to be dwelt on, with some of the theological reflections that have grown out of that passage over the Church's history of reflecting on it.

John Paul notes how the recitation of the rosary over the years gives a continuity to one's prayer life, an identity maintained in contact with God. Bits of our own life are strung like beads on the thread of our recurrent addresses to God in times of loss or happiness or struggle. "Thus the simple prayer of the rosary marks the rhythm of human life" (2). My own memories of saying the rosary run through most of my conscious life. I can remember our family saying the rosary together at my grandparents' house during Lent. In high school we said it during May (known as Mary's month). When I was at a Jesuit seminary in the 1950s, small groups of us would say it together while walking after dinner. But those shared experiences are not as vivid to me as the times when I said it alone—as when waiting for the delivery of our first child. Or walking alone at night in a strange city. Or jogging at 5 A.M. in Venice or Bologna. Or groping to disentangle beads from car keys in my pocket and breaking another (umpteenth) rosary.

Those just beginning to say the rosary will not have that backlog of associations. But the devotion's benefits are enough in themselves, and the added richness of repeated use will come in time. This aspect of the matter may sound too inner-turning or even self-centered, a charge that is made about other forms of contemplation where wholeness of the self is an aim. But Saint Augustine maintained that the search for God must take place inside one. God, he says in the *Confessions* (3.11), is "deeper in me than I am in me" *(intimior intimo meo)*. Since we are made in God's image, our own diversity-in-unity reflects God's tri-unity. The rosary is one way of entering into oneself, where he awaits us.

1. Background

IN ORDER TO SAY THE ROSARY, one does not need to know much if anything about the history of the practice. It was for a long time shrouded in legend. But it may help one's devotion to know what deep roots the practice has in the biblical, conciliar, and ecclesiastical past. Awareness that one's prayer continues that of a long line of saints and scholars may bring increased appreciation of what it means to be one member of the mystical body of Christ praying with so many other members.

1. History of the Rosary

ACCORDING TO A LEGEND once endorsed by popes and celebrated in famous paintings, the Virgin Mary appeared to Saint
Dominic, the founder of the Order of Preachers (Dominicans),
and presented him with the first rosary. That was in the
thirteenth century. Modern research has found three things
wrong with this story. *First*, early biographies and paintings of
Dominic—along with early documents of his order—do not
connect him with the rosary. The legend is not mentioned for
two centuries after his death. *Second*, the saying of repeated
Our Fathers or Hail Marys with the help of beads long pre-
dates Dominic. *Third*, the linking of contemplated gospel mysteries with the recitation of the prayers—which we consider
essential to the rosary—long postdates Dominic.

The medieval roots of the rosary lie in the effort of laypeople to have their own extended prayer, an equivalent to the
Divine Office said and sung by monks and friars. The office was
a complex set of biblical and hagiographical readings, of prayers and of hymns, each part keyed to a different time of the day
in the different seasons of the year. A briefer form of this, a *breviary*, was created for itinerant (mendicant) orders that did not
have a monastery to keep the eight different hours of the full

office. All Western Catholic priests were required to say the breviary until after the Second Vatican Council. For laypeople, something simpler was required. Books of prayers for certain *little hours* were invented, but even these were suitable only for the educated and (usually) the wealthy—a fact attested by the beautiful illustrations in the Books of Hours that are the pride of museums today. The problem of supplying a "lay office" continued. To avoid the complexity of different combinations of different kinds of prayer, the straightforward recitation of all 150 psalms was tried. When this proved too long or trying a task, the psalter was split into three parts, so fifty psalms were recited at any one time. These numbers—150, 100, and 50— would be important to the development of the rosary.

The recitation of the psalms was still a complex matter. For ordinary Christians it was important to have a prayer that could be said without using a book. Instead of reciting 150 psalms, why not just say the Our Father (Pater Noster) 150 times—shortening that number, if necessary, as the psalter had been shortened, to 100 or to 50 repetitions? The Our Father was the one prayer all Christians were supposed to know; it was in the Bible (Matthew 6.9–13), and instruction in it was part of the ancient baptismal discipline. Though the psalms were no longer being recited, the canonical numbers (150 or 100 or 50) gave this exercise the name *the Pater Noster psalter*, and it was later called *the Pater Noster rosary*. Saying the same prayer over and over required a counting device, which is what the beads provided. A set of such beads was itself called a Pater Noster, and artisans created them in workshops like those along Pater Noster Row in London.

The Hail Mary (Ave Maria) did not exist in its current form until the fifteenth century. But when it became popular, it too was said to the beads 150 (or 100, or 50) times. Soon the *Ave Maria rosary* became more popular than the Pater Noster rosary. But this exercise, like its forerunner, was still just a matter of repeating one prayer over and over. The idea of articulating the parts of the rosary to consider different episodes in the life of Christ was explored in the fourteenth century. But it was not till the early fifteenth century that a rationalized scheme for such contemplation of Christ's life became well known. The innovator was Dominic of Prussia (1382–1460), a Carthusian monk and author who was born in Poland and died at Trier.

In keeping with the psalm-based numerology of all these exercises, Dominic proposed fifty events in Christ's life for contemplation. He claims to have had a vision in which a tree had fifty leaves, each devoted to a single gospel episode. This was perhaps suggested by the "visual New Testaments" of the middle ages—paintings that portrayed the life of Christ in a series of separate panels. (Duccio's famous altarpiece in Siena devoted sixty-two of its seventy-five panels to the life of Christ.)

To keep track of the episode being meditated on, Dominic adjusted each Hail Mary to include the episode. Thus: "And blessed is the fruit of thy womb, Jesus, *whose birth was announced by the angel,*" or ". . . the fruit of thy womb, Jesus, *who was born in Bethlehem.*" These insertions are still made in some places, a practice commended by Paul VI (46) and John Paul II (33). A critic of Dominic of Prussia, the Dominican priest Alanus de Rupe (1428–1475) thought he had shortchanged the gospel by not giving the full psalter number of 150 episodes. But the practical difficulty of dealing even with fifty events led to a shortening and categorizing of episodes; by the sixteenth century they had been sorted into three sets of five episodes, each set of episodes thematically linked as glad, sad, or glorious. The number fifty was retained, since the beads of the five decades in each set numbered fifty.

It was Alanus de Rupe who, perhaps in opposition to Dominic of Prussia, popularized the story that the founder of his own order was also the initiator of the rosary prayer. His fellow Dominicans picked up this notion with enthusiasm and made it the reigning view for centuries. Alanus formed a Confraternity of the Psalter of the Glorious Virgin Mary at Douai around 1470. It soon had many chapters and imitators, making the rosary immensely popular on a broad front of the Western church. (The Eastern church has its own form of the prayer beads, usually 100, known as the *kombologion*.) It should be remembered that all this activity took place before the Reformation, so that the rosary is part of the history of Protestants as well as Catholics. Anglicans remind us that devotion to Saint Mary is not confined to Catholics, since Mary says in Luke's gospel, "I shall be called blessed down the generations" (Luke 1.48).

Unfortunately, the rosary did become a partisan symbol of Catholicism. Some religious orders wore a huge set of the beads hanging from the belts of their habits—beads not so much for actual use in prayer but as a kind of defiant emblem. Anti-Catholics sometimes mocked the devotion to mere beads. In 1906, when the British author Hilaire Belloc ran for Parliament in the Liberal Party, he spoke defiantly on the stump:

> Gentlemen, I am a Roman Catholic. As far as possible, I go to Mass every day. This [taking a rosary out of his pocket] is a rosary. As far as possible, I kneel down and tell these beads every day. If you reject me on account of my religion, I shall

thank God that he has spared me the indignity of being made your representative.

Belloc's biographer Robert Speaight observes: "After a shocked silence, there was a thunder-clap of applause."

One reason why use of the rosary became confined to Catholics was a curse that was given in the form of a blessing. From the fifteenth century on, indulgences—papal dispensations from time in purgatory—were attached to its recitation. The sale of indulgences was one reason for Luther's break with the church, and the rosary was tarred with the brush of this corrupt practice. The very idea of indulgences was tainted from the outset. The claim that the pope could give partial or total reprieves from time spent in purgatory is absurd on the face of it. Who knows what *time* would mean in purgatory—does it follow the Gregorian calendar? The offer of such a reprieve was improvised by those preaching the First Crusade (1095), when Rome had not authorized the idea and had no theological argument on which to base it. Yet the grant was so desired and clamored after—and eventually so lucrative—that lame excuses were confected for it.

Indulgences have been dying a decent death in modern times, in the quiet way the church has of forgetting embarrassments. Paul VI does not mention indulgences in his list of reasons for praying the rosary, and John Paul II says nothing of indulgences for the rosary itself, though he offers one for an appended prayer for his intentions (37). But the indulgences had their sad effect for a long time. Racing through the requisite number of prayers just to get the indulgence worked against the whole concept of contemplative calm. Besides, it was thought that the indulgence inhered in the beads themselves. If you had no beads at hand, it made no sense to say the prayers, since you got no indulgence. To add superstition to superstition, it was thought that the indulgence depended on using beads blessed by a priest. If they could be blessed by the pope himself, they would be especially potent. That is why, at papal audiences, hundreds of people held up rosaries when he blessed the crowd—some holding fistsful of many rosaries, for their family and friends. John Paul admits (28) that this can reduce the rosary to the status of a magic amulet.

My own contemporaries grew up in a culture that led to such indulgence hunting. This trend was at its worst on All Souls Day, the day after All Saints Day (All Hallows, following on Hallows Eve, Halloween). On All Souls Day, a special indulgence could be won by visiting a church—so there was a rush to duck into many churches, to tally up the indulgences. In the same way, the rosary was rattled off, as fast and as frequently as possible, to get indulgences given to its recitation. This explains why many Catholics who remember preconciliar days have sour memories of the rosary. John Paul II says (4) that such bad memories have led to "a crisis of the rosary." He, like Paul VI, has tried to remove the offensive connections with past error. Both stress the quiet and calm mood in which the rosary should be said. John Paul says (28) that the prayers, though "usually" said to the beads, can be said without them. Both popes stress freedom in the use of the prayers, recommending improvisations like the addition of clauses or other prayers, and rejecting all fetishisms regarding the physical beads themselves.

John Paul has, in this spirit, opened a welcome new chapter in the history of the rosary by adding a new set of five mysteries to the traditional fifteen. He calls these the *luminous myster-ies*, or *mysteries of light*, since they show Christ revealing the meaning of his ministry—the five are Christ's Baptism, the Marriage at Cana, the Sermon on the Mount, the Transfiguration, and the Last Supper. Adding these mysteries breaks with the psalter numerology of the devotion's past history. The use of three sets of mysteries entailed the saying of 150 Hail Marys in the decades of the whole—or 100 or 50 if one said two sets or just one. That is one reason the restricted number of mysteries was adopted in the first place. The pope has broken those confines now, since the twenty mysteries are not reducible to the old schema of 150-100-50.

Why this innovation in a deeply traditional practice? The previous list of gospel events omitted the whole of the public ministry of Jesus. The glad set covered Christ's childhood. The sad set covered his passion and death. The glorious set covered Christ's resurrection and the subsequent life of the church. This not only gave a drastically truncated version of Christ's life but—for those who said the rosary in connection with the liturgical seasons—led to an imbalance in the use of the beads. The glad mysteries were said only in the time from the beginning of Advent to the beginning of Lent. The sad mysteries were used only in Lent. That left most of the year to repetition of the glorious mysteries. Now there is a new set of meditations for the post-pentecostal time.

Of course, one does not have to say the rosary in accord with the liturgical seasons. John Paul suggests (8) another practice, the keying of different mysteries to different days of the week. But I could never remember what day called for what mysteries, even when there were only fifteen of them. Having twenty makes that even more complicated. Besides, when the recitation is attuned to the whole church's concern with the different moods of the liturgical year, this makes it transcend individual whim. One breathes, as it were, with the whole body of believers.

Yet one does not have to follow any pattern. Indeed, one does not have to say the rosary. But if one does, it should be a personal exercise as well as a communal discipline. If a mystery evokes a special response, one can dwell on it at length and spend less time on the others—or omit them altogether. At Christmastime, I repeat just the third mystery, Christ's Birth, on all five decades of the beads. The rosary is not an assignment, just a help to contemplation and to prayer. The point of having a full course of mysteries to contemplate is simply to provide a framework within which to structure one's reflection. The uses to which one puts that framework can and should differ from person to person.

Well, if that is the case, why use the beads at all? One does not have to. The ability to pray should not be limited by the accident of having the beads whenever one wants to pray the rosary. Counting the prayers is not a difficult matter for people who have ten fingers. William F. Buckley Jr. records a common occurrence for Catholics of his (and my) generation in his published diary *Overdrive*:

> Having twice checked the alarm clock, because I am due at the airport at 9 A.M., I read something about somebody and, turning off the light, remember to count on my fingers the five decades of the rosary, a lifelong habit acquired in childhood and remembered about half the time. That half of my

life, I like to think, I behave less offensively to my Maker than the other half.

Nonetheless, the fingers' transit along the beads, if one strips them of fetishistic connections, can help put one in a prayerful mood—the use of worry beads and other prayer aids indicates that. There is a kind of tactile memory evoked in their use, helping recall other times of prayer. The British author Eamon Duffy, in his book *Faith of Our Fathers*, says that the click of rosary beads brings back childhood memories of his grandmother praying through sleepless nights, with her "muttered preamble—This one is for Tom, for Molly, for Lily—as she launched on yet another decade." (Praying for different members of the family on different decades can be a useful practice.)

There is a natural symbolism in their threaded continuity. I am reminded of the fresco *Good Government* in Siena, in which the citizens hold on to a rope that goes up to the figure of Justice, a sign of linked activity and mutual support. Even better, perhaps, is Michelangelo's great figure of the angel in his *Last Judgment*, who reaches down and pulls up two risen souls using the rosary as a rope to bring them safely home. The beads can, indeed, hold us together.

2. *Elements of the Rosary*

The Physical Object

THE ROSARY IS A CIRCLET containing five groups of beads, with a pendent string of five beads and a crucifix. One begins prayer at the crucifix, on which one says the creed. One proceeds to the five beads on the pendent string—an Our Father, three Hail Marys, a Glory Be (not given a bead), and another Our Father. This last Our Father goes with the first group of beads within the circlet. Each group of ten Hail Marys (a *decade*) is preceded by an Our Father (its bead set off somewhat from the decade) and followed by a Glory Be (said without a bead of its own). One meditates on a different part of Christ's life *(mystery)* on each decade. This sounds far more complicated in description than it is in practice.

The Name

"ROSARY" COMES FROM the Latin *rosarium,* meaning "rose garden." The *rosarium* was used as a secular symbol of love in classical times, which made the fifteenth-century Dominican Alanus de Rupe reject its use for the Virgin—he retained the old designation, *Psalter of the Virgin.* But Christian usage increasingly connected the word with a rose *garland,* or chaplet of the Virgin, to suggest the circlet of beads. The Eastern equivalent of the rosary is also called a chaplet *(kombologion).* Albrecht Dürer created the most celebrated of his oil paintings, around 1500, for the German Confraternity of the Rosary in Venice. Called *The Feast of the Rose Garlands,* it shows the Virgin, the Christ child, Saint Dominic, and a flock of angels all giving out rose garlands as symbols of the rosary.

The Creed

ONE BEGINS the rosary at the pendent crucifix, by reciting the Apostles' Creed, with its Trinitarian structure:

> I BELIEVE IN GOD, THE FATHER ALMIGHTY, creator of heaven and earth.

> AND IN JESUS CHRIST, his only Son, our Lord, who was conceived by the Holy Spirit, born of the Virgin Mary, suffered under Pontius Pilate, was crucified, died, and was buried. He descended into hell; the third day he rose again from the dead; he ascended into heaven, sits at the right hand of God, the Father almighty; from thence he shall come to judge the living and the dead.

I BELIEVE IN THE HOLY SPIRIT, the holy Catholic Church, the communion of saints, the forgiveness of sins, the resurrection of the body, and life everlasting. Amen.

That is the Apostles' Creed, which we learned in catechism class as children. The Nicene Creed, said at Mass, was said in Latin when we grew up, reserved for the priest. The Apostles' Creed was the layman's creed. Now that the Mass is in English and the whole congregation recites the Nicene Creed together, I daresay more young people know it than the Apostles' Creed. Should they memorize the Apostles' Creed just for saying the rosary? Not unless they want to. Either prayer will serve. They are basically the same. The Apostles' Creed is older (second century) and simpler. The Nicene Creed is a little longer, more doctrinally complex, and more recent (fourth century).

WE BELIEVE IN ONE GOD, THE FATHER ALMIGHTY, maker of heaven and earth, of all that is seen and unseen.

WE BELIEVE IN ONE LORD, JESUS CHRIST, the only Son of God, eternally begotten of the Father, God from God, Light from Light, true God from true God, begotten, not made, one in being with the Father. Through him all things were made. For us men and for our salvation he came down from heaven. By the power of the Holy Spirit he was born of the Virgin Mary and became man. For our sake he was crucified under Pontius Pilate. He suffered, died, and was buried. On the third day he rose again in fulfillment of the scriptures. He ascended into heaven and is seated at the right hand of the Father. He will come again in glory to judge the living and the dead, and his kingdom will have no end.

WE BELIEVE IN THE HOLY SPIRIT, the Lord, the giver of
life, who proceeds from the Father and the Son. With
the Father and the Son he is worshiped and glorified.
He has spoken through the prophets. We believe in one
holy catholic and apostolic Church. We acknowledge
one baptism for the forgiveness of sins. We look for the
resurrection of the dead, and the life of the world to
come. Amen.

Both creeds grew out of baptism practices in the early
church, and reciting either creed is a way of renewing one's baptismal vows. In an ancient baptism, the baptisand was stripped
naked, then totally immersed three times in the baptismal pool.
Before the first immersion, one was asked: "Do you believe in
God the Father?" Before the second: "Do you believe in his
only son, Jesus Christ?" Before the third: "Do you believe in
the Holy Spirit?" This rebirth was into a life activated by all
three Persons of the Trinity. The Christian was urged to relive
this experience by reciting the creed daily. Saying the rosary
insures that one will say this prayer (among others).

The second clause of each creed, devoted to the birth,
death, and resurrection of the Son, is longer than the other
two, since we learn of the other two only as revealed by Jesus,
sent on his mission by the Father and sending the Spirit into
his church. Saint Paul says that going under the water reenacts
the death of Christ, as rising from it prefigures our resurrection. This fact gives the creed its dynamic character, its drama.

The Our Father

In EARLY PREPARATIONS for baptism, the creed and the Our Father were the last *secrets* of the faith *(arcana)* to be taught to the candidates. They are the basic prayers of the church, the one formulated by the Spirit, the other given by Christ in the gospel. Like the creed, the Our Father was to be recited daily—in fact, according to the early church document known as the *Didache* (circa 100 C.E.), one should say the Our Father three times daily, in honor of the Trinity. Those praying the rosary say it six times, twice the ancient suggestion. These are the rosary's deep roots.

The Jesus who teaches this prayer at Matthew 6.9–13 is praying with and in the church. The first half of the prayer glorifies the Father, as Christ regularly did. The second half is a communal plea, with emphasis on the believers' solidarity with one another:

> Give US this day
> OUR daily bread,
> And forgive US OUR debts,
> as WE forgive OUR debtors,
> And lead US not into temptation,
> but deliver US from evil.

Scholars are now agreed that this is an apocalyptic prayer, one that looks to the end-time of history, in keeping with early Christian expectations. In that setting, the clauses mean something more than, or different from, their ordinary sense now. The first clause of this prayer section has an unexampled adjective *(epiousios)* applied to bread. It is usually translated "daily" bread, since *ousios*, which follows the preposition *epi*, "upon," can come from the verb for "to be," and so *epiousios* would mean "on-being" (actual, present, daily). But *ousios* could, with equal etymological validity, come from the verb for "to come"—"the on-coming bread." In an apocalyptic context, where the messianic meal at the end of time comes first to mind, this suggests the feast God will have with his saved ones. This accounts for the emphatic "this day" *(sēmeron)*. We are asking to anticipate our homecoming, to sample even now the final blissful meal. Jesus had prompted such an anticipation at the Last Supper, when he drank *some* wine but then no more: "Solemnly I say that I shall from now on drink no more the vine's offspring until the day I drink a new wine in the reign of God" (Mark 14.23). The Lord's Prayer refers, then, to our participation in the Eucharist as a prefiguration of the feast at the end-time. That feast is regularly mentioned in the gospels:

"Happy the one who eats bread in the kingdom of God." (Luke 1.15)

"I dispose my reign for you as my Father has disposed it for me, that you eat and drink at my table." (Luke 22.29–30)

"I promise you that many will come from the East and from the West to take their place at table with Abraham, Isaac, and Jacob in heaven's reign." (Matthew 8.11)

The second clause of the Our Father, "Forgive us our debts," also has an end-time meaning. It refers to the great day of reckoning (Jeremiah 27), modeled on the Jews' jubilee years, when all debts were canceled. This is not a kind of divine bribery—if we forgive others, will you forgive us? The great final accounting, to which this looks forward, will be once-for-all omnidirectional forgiveness of outstanding grievances, to effect the great reconciliation that concludes history.

The last clause has always mystified people. Why would God lead us into temptation *(peirasmos)*? Scholarly modern versions rightly translate *Peirasmos* as "the Trial." This is a technical term in the New Testament. It refers to the tribulation that will mark the final showdown with the Prince of this World. Jesus sanctions this prayer at Mark 14.38: "Keep awake, and pray that you enter not into the Trial *[Peirasmos]*." In Revelation 3.10 the Lord says: "Because you have kept my counsel of perseverance, I will keep you from the Trial *[Peirasmos]* about to reach the whole world, putting its inhabitants to the test."

The second part of this clause parallels the first part—such repetition is the structural principle of Hebrew poetry. It should read, "Deliver us from the Evil One," not "Deliver us from evil." The genitive *ponerou* can be either neuter ("evil") or masculine ("Evil One"); but the eschatological context makes it clear that the prayer is to escape the Prince of this World, who is defeated only at the end of time. The identity of this apocalyptic figure is made clear in several places:

"Let your word be yea or be nay. One goes further at the Evil One's prompting." (Matthew 5.37)

"If one hears news of God's reign but does not absorb it, the Evil One comes and dislodges the seed that was sown in his heart." (Matthew 13.19)

"The good seed are the offspring of the reign of God; the bad seed are the offspring of the Evil One." (Matthew 13.38)

"I do not ask that you release them from the world but that you guard them from the Evil One." (John 17.15)

. . . *quench all the Evil One's fiery arrows.* (Ephesians 6.16)

He will strengthen you and fend off the Evil One. (2 Thessalonians 3.3)

You have overcome the Evil One. (1 John 2.13)

Cain was the son of the Evil One. (1 John 3.12)

The world's entire system is in thrall to the Evil One. (1 John 5.19)

Although the early church saw the end of the world as imminent, why should we reenter that frame of mind, now that we know that the world was not about to end? Well, the New Testament invites us to see eternity as continually intersecting—literally, cutting across—time. This is a synchronic, not a diachronic, faith. We are created now, at every now. Christ comes now; the Incarnation is now. The great judgment is now. "The accomplishment of everything impends" (1 Peter 4.7). Christ brought his reign with him. It is both present and to come. John Henry Newman presented the biblical view this way in his sermon "Waiting for Christ":

Up to Christ's coming in the flesh, the course of things ran straight towards that end, nearing it by every step; but now, under the gospel, that course has (if I may so speak) altered its direction as regards his second coming and runs not towards the end, but along it and on the brink of it; and is at all times equally near that great event, which, did it turn towards it, it would at once run into. Christ, then, is ever at our door; as near eighteen hundred years ago as now, and not nearer now than then; and not nearer when he comes than now. . . . This present state of things, "the present distress" as St. Paul calls it, is ever *close upon* the next world, and resolves itself into it. As when a man is given over, he may die any moment, yet lingers; as an implement of war may any moment explode, and must at some time; as we listen for a clock to strike, and at length it surprises us; as a crumbling arch hangs, we know not how, and is not safe to pass under; so creeps on this feeble weary world, and one day, before we know where we are, it will end.

That is the attitude expressed in the Our Father.

The Hail Mary

AFTER THE CREED and the first Our Father, still on the pendent string of beads, we say three Hail Marys. Some have said that these stand for the three theological virtues—the faith, hope, and love described by Saint Paul at 1 Corinthians 13.13—but coming as they do after the Trinitarian creed and before the Trinitarian Glory Be, they are clearly marked off to honor the persons of the Trinity, into whose unity we are baptized.

The Hail Mary itself did not exist in its current form until the fifteenth century. Before that, people just repeated its opening salutation as a kind of doxology (a "Glory be to Mary"). This was the angel's greeting at the Annunciation: "Hail Mary, full of grace, the Lord is with thee" (Luke 1.28). The devout would bow (or even genuflect) with each greeting, as if re-enacting the angel's address. (Repeated bowings of respect exist in other religions.) In time, another salutation was added to the first one—Elizabeth's words when her cousin Mary visited her: "Blessed is the fruit of thy womb" (Luke 1.42). In the thirteenth century, the word "Jesus" was added after "fruit of thy womb." Finally, a prayer was added to the acclamation: "Holy Mary, Mother of God, pray for us sinners now and at the hour of our death." The whole prayer was being said in the fifteenth century, and was added to the priests' breviary in the sixteenth. Compared with the creed and the Our Father, therefore, this prayer is a relative newcomer, though a very popular one. Adding the prayer to the acclamation put "Jesus" at the center of the whole. John Paul II calls this word the "hinge" of the whole prayer, which turns around the child Mary bore and continues to bring to us.

The Doxology (Glory Be)

THIS SHORT PRAYER is said after each string of Hail Marys—after the initial three and then after each group of ten:

> Glory be to the Father, and to the Son, and to the Holy Spirit, as it was in the beginning, is now, and ever shall be.

It is called a doxology because it gives glory (*doxa* in Greek) to God. Such acclamations are common in most religions (for instance, "Great is Allah") and are frequent in Jewish prayers, where such praise of the Lord goes by the general name *hallel*. The doxology used in the rosary (and in other places, like the liturgical hours) is called the Lesser Doxology, to distinguish it from the Greater Doxology, an ancient hymn recited as part of the Ordinary of the Mass:

> Glory to God in the highest, and peace to his people on earth. Lord God, heavenly King, almighty God and Father, we worship you, we give you thanks, we praise you for your glory.
>
> Lord Jesus Christ, only Son of the Father, Lord God, Lamb of God, you take away the sin of the world. Have mercy on us. You are seated at the right hand of the Father. Receive our prayer.
>
> For you alone are the Holy One, you alone are the Lord, you alone are the Most High, Jesus Christ, with the Holy Spirit, in the glory of God the Father.

The Greater Doxology is based on the angels' proclamation at the birth of Christ: "Glory to God in the highest" (Luke 2.14). The Lesser is based on the baptism formula at Matthew 28.19: "Baptize them in the name of the Father and the Son and the Holy Spirit." Both resemble the creeds in their Trinitarian structure. The Lesser repeats the invocation of the three Persons in its closing phrases:

> as it was in the beginning [Father],
> is now [Son],
> and ever shall be [Holy Spirit]

It is this Trinitarian aspect of the acclamation that sets Christian doxologies apart from those in other monotheistic religions. We find the same thing in the doxology of the Eucharistic Prayer at Mass:

Through him, with him, in him, in the unity of the Holy
Spirit, all glory and honor is yours, almighty Father, for
ever and ever.

These doxologies descend from fourth-century affirmations
of the faith against Arian and other heresies that denied the
equality of the Persons of the Trinity.

Aids to Reflection

EACH CHRISTIAN will have his or her associations with episodes in the gospel narratives. The principal ones, of course,
are the passages in scripture that relate the event. Ancillary
readings have been suggested in various books on the rosary.
It is best for each person to turn to the memory of what was
impressive in his or her past life of prayer. I turn most often
to the writings of Saint Augustine, Gilbert Chesterton, or Father Raymond Brown, but they are mentioned in what follows
just to jog the memories of people who have their own favorite
associations.

Perhaps the most time-tested aids to meditation are visual
images. It was mentioned earlier that Dominic of Prussia was
probably influenced in his choice of fifty gospel episodes by the
panel paintings of his day. The influence became reciprocal after the rosary took the form of three cycles of mysteries.
Groups of paintings were arranged to follow their sequence.
The use of visual images to help one meditate on the gospel
event is recommended by John Paul II (29): "Using a suitable
icon to portray it [the particular mystery] is, as it were, to open
up a scenario on which to focus our attention." He refers to
the way Saint Ignatius Loyola urged those meditating on a par-

ticular moment in Christ's life to form a representation of the scene (he called it a *compositio loci*). One artist who can prove useful for this purpose is Tintoretto.

TINTORETTO

His name was Jacopo Robusti, but he was nicknamed Tintoretto ("Little Dyer") because his father was a dyer of fabrics *(tintore)* for rich Venetian gowns and furnishings. Jacopo was a Venetian through and through, born and dying in that city (1518–1594), and spending his whole career in the service of its governmental and church buildings. A younger contemporary of Michelangelo and Titian, he strove to combine the draftsmanship of the former with the color of the latter.

He is best known for the flowing energy of his figures, large and muscular bodies that move with the lightness of ballet dancers. His angels are aeronautical wonders, flying in every possible foreshortened configuration. He is said to have modeled three-dimensional figures and hung them in different poses, making them interact in sequences of complex choreography. He made his drawings from these models, then used the drawings to create his paintings. He composed at a furious rate, with members of his family (including his daughter) and other expert assistants filling out the designs he threw off so brilliantly.

His deepest meditations were on the mystery of the Eucharist, as prefigured in the Jewish scripture and as connected with the Passion and death of Jesus. He was a favorite of the Eucharistic confraternities of Venice, which had altars in many churches throughout the city. For many of them he created profound and varied paintings of the Last Supper. The Christ in his pictures is a commanding figure of mystery, his face often shadowed and limned with a glow that is less the conventional halo than an emanation of spiritual intensity. His major cycle of scriptural paintings was executed for the Confraternity of Saint Roch, whose building he turned into one vast mystical dramatization of the Eucharist's meaning.

II. The Joyful Mysteries

THE FIVE GLAD MYSTERIES are all taken from the gospel of Saint Luke, and they make the only set of five in which Mary is an active participant in each decade. Luke's theological interpretation of the childhood of Jesus emphasizes how deeply rooted in Jewish life, family, society, history, teachings, and poetry is the Christ who came to save all mankind. This is the more surprising since Luke was very likely a Gentile Christian; he wrote the best Greek in the New Testament. Luke shows how important to the early church was a recognition of the Jewish context of Jesus' life and work. The joyous mysteries are ecumenical mysteries, renewing our own deep connection with and indebtedness to the Jews' continuing witness to the one God.

1. ANNUNCIATION

The angel Gabriel was sent by God to a town in Galilee called Nazareth, to a maiden betrothed to a man named Joseph, of David's line. The maiden's name was Mary. Going in to her, the angel said, "Hail, Highly Favored, the Lord is with you." She was stunned by this greeting, and tried to make sense of it.

The angel continued, "Fear not, Mary. You are favored by God. For you shall carry in your womb and bring to birth a child, and shall call him Jesus. Great he shall be, called the High One's son. God shall give him his forebear David's throne, to be the eternal king of Jacob's house, in a never-ending reign."

Mary said, "How can this happen to me, who have not lain with a man?"

The angel answered: "The Holy Spirit will come upon you, and the power of the Most High will cover you with light—which is why the child of this birth shall be holy, the acknowledged Son of God. And your cousin Elizabeth, old as she is and considered barren, has conceived a child and is in the sixth month—since nothing can be called impossible for God."

Mary answered: "I attend on the Lord. Let it happen as you say."

(Luke 1.26–38)

THE MISSION OF CHRIST, laid out here, takes place in Jewish salvation history—the emphasis is on the throne of David, the house of Jacob. More than that, Luke has patterned the angel's words on the announcements that heralded the birth of great biblical figures (Moses, Samuel, Ishmael, Isaac), or the forecasts of David's reign (2 Samuel 7.16), or the parallel birth of the Baptist. But Jesus' birth, though in this line, is a far greater event. To signal that, it is emphasized that he is born of a virgin. This fact is acknowledged not only in Luke's gospel but in Matthew's gospel, and in the Apostles' Creed. It was a tradition, therefore, that antedated them all in Christian belief. Christ was born of the Holy Spirit as well as of Mary.

This is not a gynecological datum but a theological one. As Jesuit Father Joseph Fitzmyer says, it "is never presented in any biological sense." And Sulpician Father Raymond Brown:

All Christians should be wary of any implication that the conception of Jesus in wedlock would detract from his nobility or Mary's sanctity. In its origins, the virginal conception shows no traces whatsoever of antisexual bias, and should not be made to support one. For the evangelists it was a visible sign of God's gracious intervention in connection with the becoming of His Son; in no way did that intervention make ordinary conception in marriage less holy.

What is emphasized in the theological sense of virginity is the fresh start being given to history, God's breaking in on the run of human affairs with new things to be seen and done. John Donne put it this way in his poem to Mary ("Annunciation"):

> Ere by the spheres time was created, thou
> Wast in his mind, who is thy Son and Brother—
> Whom thou conceiv'st, conceived. Yea, thou art now
> Thy Maker's maker, and thy Father's mother.
> Thou hast light in dark, and shut'st in little room,
> Immensity cloistered in thy dear womb.

Mary's acceptance of this mystery is a model for us in staying open to the incursions of the divine into our life. Christ will even make it possible for those in his mystical body to have their own kind of virgin birth, a participation in his: "Any who accepted him, who placed their trust in his name, he gave the rank of God's children, conceived not from human descent or fleshly desire but from God" (John 1.12–13).

In our prayer to Mary we can replicate in some small way the bringing forth of Christ. That is the meaning Saint Augustine found in the Annunciation: "You who are astonished at what is wrought in Mary's body, imitate it in your soul's inmost chamber. Sincerely believe in God's justice, and you conceive Christ. Bring forth words of salvation, and you have given birth to Christ" (Sermon 191). The Jesuit poet Gerard Manley Hopkins put the same truth even more dramatically:

Of her flesh he took flesh—
He does take fresh and fresh
(Though much the mystery how)
Not flesh but spirit now,
And makes (O marvelous!)
New Nazareths in us,
Where she shall yet conceive
Him, morning, noon and eve,
New Bethlems, and he born
There, evening, noon and morn.
Bethlem or Nazareth,
Men here may draw like breath
More Christ and baffle death.

We are taken, by the mystery of our rebirth into Christ in baptism, into the inner drama of the Incarnation, receiving Christ along with Mary and bringing him forth to others in our risen life.

TINTORETTO

Tintoretto is unlike most painters who treat the Annunciation. He does not show the angel standing mildly at the door of Mary's home, a lily in his hand. This Gabriel swoops over her shattered threshold in spiraling flight. The dove of the Holy Spirit plunges like a dive bomber, trailing a squadron of fighter angels. And Mary is not the porcelain doll of some paintings, prim on her knees or seated in prayer, immobile in a perfect state of passive acceptance. She is a workingwoman. She has abruptly twisted around from her spinning, "stunned" as the gospel says, dropping her distaff. And Joseph is not discreetly absent, but hard at work in the lumberyard outside the door (which resembles a Venetian gondola yard, a *squero*).

Here is drama, not the serenity of most such pictures—the calm maiden, the unrumpled bed, the symbols of purity: enclosed garden, lilies, translucent vases. The working couple repeat the iconography of Adam and Eve expelled from the garden, Adam laboring the land and Eve with a distaff. Mary is the second Eve, about to be lifted from the plight of the old Eve. Her crumbling home draws on nativity iconography, where the child is born in a classical ruin, to symbolize the ending of the old order. So here we have a decaying Venetian palazzo. It has plaster falling from its exposed brick walls, a disintegrating straw chair, and clutter at the door. The horizon shows the glow of a setting sun, about to bring night back. But a new and different light is shed from the dove, illuminating the angel and Mary. The incursion of God into ordinary life is presented with a depth of pictorial references that matches tradition with originality, just the right note for this divine break-in.

2. VISITATION

At that point Mary was quick to set out for the hills, for a city of Judah. Entering the home of Zachariah, she greeted Elizabeth. At the very instant when Elizabeth heard Mary greet her, the child stirred in her womb, and Elizabeth, filled with the Holy Spirit, lifted a loud cry: "Blessed are you among women, and blessed the fruit of your womb. But why should my Lord's mother come to me? Just think, the moment your greeting reached my ears, the child stirred in my womb with happiness. Happy, then, the woman who has trust in the Lord's promise to her."

(Luke 1.39–45)

As soon as Mary learns that her cousin is pregnant in her very old age, she hastens to her. There would be an urgent need for these women, caught up in mysterious happenings, to compare notes, to ponder the wondrous burdens committed to them. Luke presents the result of these ponderings as the poetic interchange between them. He is continuing his emphasis on Jewish family ties and religious thinking. The event formulates, in theological symbol, the relationship between these two women's two sons, the interactive missions committed to John and to Jesus. John recognizes Jesus even while both are in the womb—as a prophecy of the way he will recognize Jesus as his successor, as the one who will take his Jewish reform movement and transform it and transcend it. Just as Elizabeth wonders that Mary "should come to me," John will wonder that Jesus "should come to me" for baptism (Matthew 3.14). The humility of Mary's approach to Elizabeth will be repeated in Jesus' humble approach to John at the river Jordan.

Mary is greeted as a victorious Jewish heroine by Elizabeth, who repeats the biblical greetings to Jael and Judith, women who slew enemies of Israel. Deborah proclaims at Judges 5.24: "Blessed among women be Jael." And Judith's father says:

"Blessed are you among all women on earth" (Judith 13.18). This is also like Moses' blessing on an observant Israel: "Blessed is the fruit of your body" (Deuteronomy 28.4). Mary is an embodiment of the Christian people, of its triumph over death, so she sings a victory song based on the Hebrew canticles. Her Magnificat resembles the Magnificat of Hannah at 1 Samuel 2.1, which begins:

> *My heart rejoices in the Lord,*
> *in the Lord I now hold my head high.*

It resembles, as well, the Magnificat of Judith (13.11):

> *God, even our God, is with us,*
> *to show his power yet in Jerusalem,*
> *and his forces against the enemy,*
> *as he has even done this day.*

Mary says:

> *My soul expands toward the Lord,*
> *my spirit has found joy in God who saves me,*
> *who looked from on high to his low servant,*
> *that I should be called blessed down the generations,*
> *for Power itself has expanded me,*
> *according to his name's holiness.*
>
> *His mercy runs from each to the next generation,*
> *for those who hold him in awe.*
> *He has flexed his right arm's power,*
> *and swept off pride's mad dreamers,*
> *he has brought down the lofty from their thrones,*

and lifted up those under them,
filling abundantly whoever hungers,
sending the rich off destitute.

For he has taken up his servant Israel's cause
in memory of mercies past,
According to the word he gave our fathers,
to Abraham and all his large descent.

(Luke 1.46–55)

Augustine admonishes us that we cannot "magnify" God, make him any greater than he is. All we can do is open our hearts to an increased awe and love, to take in more of that greatness, to "hold him in awe" as Mary says.

Some scholars think the Magnificat was originally a Hebrew poem given a Christian use. But Fathers Brown and Fitzmyer think it is a Christian poem that Luke puts in Mary's mouth to show that the church speaks through her, its symbol and embodiment. In either case, there is continuity with the Jewish past. Mary takes her place in the long line of Jewish women who heroically stood up for their people. We pray to her and with her, as and in the church that we and she are.

TINTORETTO

Tintoretto takes seriously what the gospel says, that Mary "set out for the hills." Mary in his painting is toiling up a steep approach toward Elizabeth, a physical presentment of her humility in coming to the aid of her cousin. In most paintings of the Visitation, only the two women are present. But here each is attended by her husband, Joseph on the left, Zachariah on the right. Mary hastens ahead of Joseph in her eagerness to reach Elizabeth. Tintoretto likes to stress the human context of divine actions, and the whole point of the Visitation is that Mary was part of a family-centered culture of worship.

Still, it is the two women who are foremost. The support they give each other, their clinging to each other, shows what strength they must give to and take from their relationship as they face the strange new world they are carrying in their wombs. This decade can be especially meaningful when said by one whose family faces problems.

3. NATIVITY

While they were there [in Bethlehem], she reached the term of her pregnancy and gave birth to a son, her firstborn, and straitened his limbs in bands, and laid him in a hay trough [phatnē], *since there was no place for them in the lodging.*

(Luke 2.6–7)

CHRISTMAS puts in the starkest terms the wonder of the Incarnation (literally, the enfleshment) of God, and it is Mary's flesh that the Second Person of the Trinity takes. Since all baptized Christians are members of Christ's mystical body, we too are sons of Mary's flesh. The Incarnation is the boldest—one can almost say the most blasphemous—claim made by Christianity. The church knew at once how breathtaking this notion is. One of the very earliest Christian texts is the hymn quoted by the earliest author in the New Testament, Saint Paul. He could use the already existing hymn to urge peace upon his fellows. Saint Paul put it in all its audacity:

> *Put your mind in Christ's when dealing with one another—for*
> *he, having the divine nature from the outset,*
> *thinking it no usurpation to be held God's equal,*
> *emptied himself out into the nature of a slave,*
> *becoming like to man.*
> *And in man's shape, he lowered himself,*
> *so obedient as to die, by death on a cross.*
> *For this God has exalted him,*
> *favored his name over all names,*

that at the name of Jesus all knees shall bend,
above the earth, upon the earth, and below the earth,
and every tongue shall acknowledge
that Jesus is the Lord Christ, to the glory of God the Father.

(Philippians 2.5–11)

The idea of God becoming man seems impossible, even to some Christians. Chesterton answers a critic who points out that impossibility:

He laboriously explains the difficulty which we have always defiantly and almost derisively exaggerated; and mildly condemns as improbable something that we have almost madly exalted as incredible; as something that would be much too good to be true, except that it is true. When that contrast between the cosmic creation and the little local infancy has been repeated, reiterated, underlined, emphasized, exulted in, sung, shouted, roared, not to say howled, in a hundred thousand hymns, carols, rhymes, rituals, pictures, poems, and popular sermons, it may be suggested that we hardly need a higher critic to draw our attention to something a little odd about it.

The scene at the crib has its center in the mother and child. Those who think attention to Mary is somehow stolen from Jesus do not realize how pivotal Mary was in defining the reality of Jesus. From the early struggles with heresy, it was her role to stand between some who thought Christ not fully human and some who thought him not fully divine. These opposite errors were confounded in the person of Mary. The concept of God-in-the-flesh can never get far from the flesh of Mary, as

Saint Augustine keeps reminding us: "The newborn child, not ready for adult food, has it mediated to him through his mother's flesh, in the form of milk—so the Lord, to transmit to us the milk of his wisdom, clothes it in his own flesh." (On Psalm 30.)

God's joining the family, as it were—by the intense topsey-turveydom of the Incarnation—is put this way by Chesterton, in his poem on the titles of the Litany of Mary, when he addresses her as Star of Morning:

> Star of His morning, that unfallen Star,
> In the strange starry overturn of space
> When earth and sky changed places for an hour,
> And heaven looked upwards in a human face.

Christmas is the most human of feasts because of the lowly circumstances of Christ's birth. The outcast family, for which there was no room in the lodging, is welcomed by the shepherds, and then by those who hear the heavenly news from the shepherds (the first human preachers of the Incarnation):

> *There were shepherds nearby, tending their flock, taking night watches in their turn. The Lord's angel took his stand before them, and the Lord's glory bathed them in light, filling them with deep fear. But the angel told them, "Fear not! I bring you news of a deep joy for all the people. This day is your savior born for you, and this is the sign of it: You will find a newborn, in his straitening clothes, who lies in a hay trough."*
>
> *All at once the angel was joined by a number of the heavenly ranks praising God in these words: "Glory in the heights to God, and peace to those he favors."*

> *And once the angels had left them, returning to heaven, the shepherds said to one another: "Go we to Bethlehem, to see the fulfillment of this word the Lord has given us." They hurried there and found Mary with Joseph, and the child lying in the hay trough. After seeing them, they revealed to others what they had heard about this child. They were all astonished at what the shepherds told them; and Mary kept these things for inner scrutiny, sifting them in her heart. The shepherds went off glorifying and praising God for all they had seen and heard in fulfillment of God's word.*
>
> (Luke 2.8–20)

God sneaks quietly into the world, welcomed by the obscure, the forgotten. We are told that he will return at the endtime "like a thief in the night" (1 Thessalonians 5.2). In his first coming, too, the secret is hidden away from the great ones of the world, but "revealed to simple people" (Luke 10.21). One must become a child to see how God became a child.

TINTORETTO

The convention of showing the nativity in a ruined classical structure has already been referred to. Tintoretto makes this a ruined farm, close to the circumstances of the first people to learn of the Incarnation from the shepherds. Unlike the treatment of this ruin in Tintoretto's *Annunciation*, where the sun is setting behind the scene in a muffled way, the new day in this *Nativity* is anticipated by the golden red clouds of angels peering through the latticework of the old barn's roof.

The people who have heard the good news rush aid to the newborn. One woman has even expressed her own milk into a bowl, to augment the Virgin's nursing. What Tintoretto presents here, as no other painter has, is the marvel that God made himself dependent on us. Mary and Joseph, poor themselves, need the support of the poor. With the generosity of shared goods, the neighbors bring sustenance—eggs, poultry, bread—to the travel-weary parents and their vulnerable newborn.

The whole barn is a manger, whose hay the ass is eating while the ox lies in it. They take up the center of the picture, where Mary and the Child are normally seen. Mary is placed off to the right, to show how important is the chain of people, running up from the lower right to the upper left, a veritable bucket brigade of help arriving just in time. Birth into the human community could not be better expressed.

4. PRESENTATION IN THE TEMPLE

When the time had lapsed for their purification according to Mosaic law, they took the child up to Jerusalem, to offer him to the Lord, as the Law of the Lord prescribes—"Every male who comes first from the womb shall be set apart for the Lord." And they sacrificed, as well, following the Law—"a pair of doves or two young pigeons."

A man happened to be in Jerusalem, a certain Simeon, observant and pious, who had looked for the comforting of Israel, inspired by the Holy Spirit—it had been foretold him by the Holy Spirit that he would not see death before he had seen the Anointed of the Lord. It was the Spirit who led him to the temple. At the entry of the parents to perform the ceremony required by the Law, Simeon took the child in his arms, blessed God, and said:

"Now, Master, you may let me go
   in peace, with your promise kept.
My eyes behold the rescue you send,
   for all people to see plainly,
a light to be shown to all nations,
   and an honor to your people, Israel."

The father and mother were astounded at what was being said about the child. Simeon blessed them and said to Mary, the child's mother:

"This very child will cause many in Israel to fall or to rise;
   he will be a sign of contradiction.
A sword shall pass through your own heart,
   and the minds of many shall be laid bare."

When they had completed all the requirements of the Law of the Lord, they returned to Galilee, to the city of Nazareth.

(Luke 2.22–33, 39)

LUKE HAS COMBINED here two ceremonies that were originally separate—the dedication of the firstborn male and the purification of Mary from ritual pollution after childbirth. The first involved a temple payment but did not require performance at the temple. The second required a visit in the pure state to the temple, but not if one resided away from Jerusalem. Luke combines the two duties, and has them discharged at the temple, since he is emphasizing the temple piety of Jesus. Over and over in this brief passage Luke notes how exactly the Law was being observed. The first Christians maintained the Law under James the brother of the Lord; and though a break from the temple came, either at the destruction of the temple in 70 c.e. or just before it, Luke is making clear what Jesus himself said (Matthew 5.17): "Think not I have come to cancel the Law or the prophets; I come not to cancel but to complete the Law."

That this completion will involve wrenching changes Luke indicates by the prophecy of Simeon, that Jesus will be a sign of contradiction, revealing the set of different minds. This is what neither Joseph nor Mary can understand. Their own piety foresees no change in the Law they have observed all their life.

The fact that Simeon is observant, though the Spirit frees him to see the possibility of new challenges, is underlined by the addition of another pious person's prophetic response to Jesus.

> *A woman prophet was there as well, Anna the daughter of Phanuel, of Asher's tribe—an aged woman who had lived seven years with a husband after her marriage as a girl, and lived afterward as a widow, now having reached her eighty-fourth year. She never left the temple, but was always worshiping there with prayers and fasts. Happening to be there at this very moment, she gave thanks to God, and spoke of the child to everyone who was hoping for Israel to be free.*
>
> (Luke 2.36–38)

Mary and Joseph do not know what to make of the glorious but clouded foresight of these Jewish seers. In fact, one may wonder why this event is included in the joyous mysteries, since Mary is told that her soul will be pierced by a sword. That ominous note takes place, however, in the context of a joyful fulfillment of the Law that bound Jews to God. There is a bittersweet aspect to the joyous mysteries, just as there will be a sweet-bitter point to the sorrowful mysteries. The former look ahead to the mission of the Incarnation—to the death of Jesus for mankind—as the latter look forward to the resurrection. Artists and preachers have mingled these strands, as the scripture does. The Incarnation implies all the fatalities of being human—the joys in sorrow and sorrows in joy, the reciprocal dynamics of life and death. No one could put this better than Saint Augustine. In Sermon 191, he wrote:

Man's maker was made man—that he who guides the Milky Way might take milk at his mother's breast, that the Bread might hunger, the Fountain thirst, the Light sleep, the Way be tired on its journey; that Truth might be accused by false witness, the Teacher be beaten with whips, the Foundation be suspended on wood; that Strength might grow weak, that the Healer might be wounded, that Life might die.

TINTORETTO

Tintoretto lays the same emphasis on the temple that Luke does. The high priest presides in all the majesty of the setting. Joseph, seated at the left, has brought the offering of doves. Two of them lie under the child on the altar. The stairs Mary has mounted recall the steps to the temple shown in many pictures of her, in her own childhood, being committed to the care of the temple priests. In the *Golden Legend*, the source of all those paintings, her relationship with the temple was an early and entire dedication of herself. It is not surprising, then, that she now offers her son to God's service, eagerly and completely. She looks across the single dramatic candle, since the feast of the Purification (February 2) was known in the past as Candlemas, for the single candle borne by each worshiper in procession—paradoxical candles, as Chesterton put it, "to purify the Pure."

5. FINDING IN THE TEMPLE

His parents went yearly to Jerusalem for the Passover feast. When he turned twelve, they went to the feast as usual. When they had completed their observances and were on the return journey, the boy Jesus stayed behind without his parents knowing it. Thinking he was part of the return party, they traveled a day before they searched for him among their friends and relatives. When they could not find him, they returned to Jerusalem and searched for him there. It took three days for them to find him, in the temple, seated there, surrounded by scholars, listening to them and asking them questions. All who heard him were astounded by his intelligence and his responses.

When his parents saw him, they were dumbfounded, and his mother asked him, "How, my son, could you treat us this way? Your father and I have been searching for you in anguish." He responded: "Why were you searching for me? Do you not realize that I must be at my Father's?"

They did not understand what he told them, but he returned with them and reached Nazareth, and obeyed them there. But his mother kept all he had said for close scrutiny in her heart. Jesus grew up mentally and physically, favored by God and by men.

(Luke 2.41–52)

THIS IS ANOTHER of the bittersweet episodes included in the joyous mysteries. There is, of course, the joy of finding a lost child; but it was preceded by five days of anguish (a day's journey out from Jerusalem, a day's return, and three days of search after they reached Jerusalem). Jesus is twelve, reaching adolescence, a fact that is emphasized by Luke when he speaks of his maturation in mind and body. This episode is Luke's synecdoche (part for whole) of the "hidden life" of Jesus, before his public ministry began. The bewilderment of his parents, dramatized here, was obviously a continuing condition, suggested by Mary's inner scrutiny of all her son said. (Only one time is mentioned in this scene, but Luke makes her pondering a continuous process.)

Most parents find their children becoming, in some measure, a mystery to them when they reach adolescence. But some few have a deeper trial, the ones whose child is marked out for greatness, who has some premonition of his or her own destiny. There is a sense that the youth is already living some larger life, on a plane removed from the limits of his or her immediate surroundings. Such youngsters are already astounding their elders—as Jesus impresses the scholars of the Law—by what they know and do. The young Napoleon, the young Mozart, the young Michelangelo—already as teens they were following a distant star. Parents look on these prodigies with a mix of pride and misgiving. Is the youth launching out into a world where they cannot follow, cannot be of help, perhaps cannot even comprehend? We can only imagine how the parents of Jesus must have wondered at his prayer, his study, his immersion in the Law, his communication with his Father. What did it all mean? Where was it all going? The more we study Luke's presentation of these questions in a kind of parable, the more appropriate his symbolism becomes. Jesus was removed from his parents, but not really; was with scholars in a strange place, but not really; was inside his culture, but not really. No wonder "his parents did not understand what he told them." Jesus in the temple was a mystery within a mystery. In that sense, he was found, but not really.

TINTORETTO

This is an early work, the painting of a young man by a young man—as we can see from the self-portrait included in it. The young Tintoretto is the boy looking out at us, the fourth head from the left side of the picture. The painter follows the text, which says that Jesus is surrounded by the scholars. He sits in a circle completed by us, the spectators, who look at him far off, removed, behind a barricade of books, weighty with the accumulation of wisdom and revelation. Mary stands to the left, out of place in this male gathering of the learned, looking at the child that is moving away from her. Yet even at this remove he reaches his hands out to her in greeting, asking if she did not realize where he must be. Mother and son communicate, but across a growing distance. Any parent must understand.

iii. The Luminous Mysteries

THESE ARE THE FIVE MYSTERIES added by Pope John Paul II, bringing the public ministry into the gospel episodes contemplated in the rosary. This is so logical an addition that one wonders why it was not made before. After all, the public ministry covers the longest part of each gospel. Omitting it gave a severely truncated picture of Christ's life. John Paul calls these the "mysteries of light" because they show Jesus teaching, whether by word, example, or symbol. What he teaches is endlessly rich, and each one praying will take different parts of an episode to heart for private meditation.

1. BAPTISM OF JESUS

Then Jesus, coming from Galilee to the Jordan, approached John to be baptized by him. John would have prevented this, saying: "I need baptism from you, yet you come to me?" Jesus answered him, "Bear with this for now—we must fill all requirements." So John complied. But as soon as Jesus, baptized, came up out of the water, the heavens parted, he saw God's Spirit coming down to him as a dove to light upon him, and a voice spoke from heaven: "This is my Son, the object of my love, who delights me."

(Matthew 3.13–17)

THIS IS A PARTICULARLY mysterious mystery, with two aspects. First, why was Jesus, who was without sin, baptized for the cleansing from sin? And second, why did Jesus not baptize during his public ministry (John 4.2), though baptism was required for all Christians after his death? In the three Synoptic Gospels, Jesus' followers perform no baptisms. In the Gospel of John, the followers baptize but Jesus does not (John 4.2). Raymond Brown concludes that the disciples were performing John the Baptist's renewable cleansing, not Christian baptism as that was understood after the death of Christ. The sacrament of baptism is normally understood to have been instituted by Christ at his ascension (Matthew 28.19).

From early times Christ's baptism has been taken as a symbol of his death. Christ will speak of his later Passion as a baptism none can share with him: "Are you able to drink the cup I drink, be baptized with the baptism that will baptize me?" (Mark 10.38). Until that later death-baptism (which is foreshadowed by this descent into the water) took place, a full forgiveness of sin could not be given to the faithful. We are told at John 7.39 that "the Spirit did not come because Jesus had not yet been glorified," from which the theologian Oscar

Cullmann concludes that "Christian baptism becomes possible only from the moment when these salvation events are completed."

John's baptism was unlike the ritual cleansings repeated on specific occasions by the Jews. It was an act of repentance and reform that looked to the imminent approach of the end-time (the final baptism by fire). Jesus endorses the validity of this as general preparation for the coming of the kingdom in his own preaching career. The early fathers said that Christ, so far from being cleansed himself, "cleansed the waters" by his baptism (Ignatius of Antioch to the Ephesians 18.1, circa 100). That is, he prepared the natural means for the ablution to be won by his passion. There is also an element of exorcism that foretells the renunciation of the devil and all his works in later baptism. That this is a preparatory baptism is signaled by Jesus' words "Bear with this for now," and also by John's statement "I baptize with water, but he who comes after me will baptize with the Holy Spirit and with fire" (Matthew 3.11).

The connection between descent into the waters and death is something Saint Paul would emphasize in his teachings on baptism—though he did not normally perform baptisms himself (1 Corinthians 1.14)—and the right of all Christians to baptize has been retained vestigially even now. Baptism for Paul was a dying into Christ:

> How can you not know that when we were baptized into Christ, we were baptized into his death? We were buried with him by this baptism into death, and just as Christ was raised from death in the splendor of his Father, so shall we stride off with a new life.
>
> (Romans 6.3–4)

As we reenact Christ's death in baptism, so he preenacted it in his own baptism. Baptism in the early centuries involved a total stripping of the catechumen, descent into the baptismal pool, and three total immersions (for the three days of Christ's death, Good Friday to Easter inclusively). The early Christians were also urged to repeat their baptismal vows often, even daily. We can do that while saying this mystery of light.

TINTORETTO

Tintoretto, who has an amazing grasp of the theology behind the events he is depicting, gives a powerful suggestion here of Jesus' baptism as foretelling his passion and death. Jesus does not stand peacefully upright as in many presentations of the baptism (most famously, perhaps, Piero della Francesca's). He bends forward as if falling on the Way of the Cross. The powerful inclination of the body resembles that seen in Tintoretto's picture of Christ's scourging (see the illustration to the second sorrowful mystery). He has taken on the whole load of the world's sin in this act. The dove hovers, ready to descend when he comes from the water, as the promise of resurrection is seen in Tintoretto's painting of the crucifixion (see the illustration to the fifth sorrowful mystery). John's reluctance to baptize his Lord is also suggested in his cautious, almost questioning, performance of the rite. He twists around, away from what he feels too awed to do. The whole work has a quiet drama of the ominous.

2. MARRIAGE AT CANA

Two days later, a wedding took place at Cana in Galilee, attended by the mother of Jesus, who was also invited, along with his followers. When the wine ran out, the mother of Jesus said, "They are out of wine." He responded: "Woman, why is your worry mine?—My time is not yet come." His mother told the servants, "Whatever thing he tells you, do that." There happened to be six stone water vessels at hand, the kind used for Jewish purifications, capable of holding fifteen to twenty-five gallons. Jesus told them, "Fill the water vessels," and they filled them to the top. He then said, "Ladle some out and take it to the steward," and they took it to him. The steward tasted the wine that had been water, not knowing its source, since only the servants who poured the water could know. The steward called to the bridegroom and told him: "Everyone first puts the best wine out, and the poorer kind only after people have been drinking. But you have kept the best wine for this moment." Cana in Galilee, then, marked the beginning of Jesus' signs, to make his glory clear, so that his followers believed in him.

(John 2.1–11)

A PIOUS INTERPRETATION of this episode makes it demonstrate the power of Mary as an intercessor. When she asks, her son complies. But this ignores the shocking response Jesus gives her, one not to be softened or ignored. Raymond Brown says that Jesus refuses to act in accord with Mary's (implied) request:

> The suggestion must be rejected that the hour of miracles was advanced by Jesus at Mary's request, for in Johannine thought the hour is not in Jesus' control but in that of the Father.... Before he does perform this sign, Jesus must make clear his refusal of Mary's intervention; she cannot have any role in his ministry; his signs must reflect his Father's sovereignty, and not any human or family agency.

Augustine had said the same thing in *Interpreting John's Gospel* (8):

> Just as Jesus was both David's son and his lord—David's son in the flesh, David's lord in his divinity—so was he Mary's son in the flesh, Mary's lord in his divinity. Because she was

not the mother of his divinity, and the miracle she was asking for had to be worked through his divinity, he answered her, "Why should your worry, woman, be mine?"

Jesus' time (literally "hour") is frequently invoked by John. It refers to the Father's plan for his life, culminating in the death and Resurrection. At John 7.30, there is an attempt to arrest Jesus, but it fails "because his time had not yet arrived." But at the Last Supper it is said that "the time had arrived for him to leave the world, going to his Father" (13.1). As he moves toward that death, his family is shunted aside: he recognized only one claim upon him—his heavenly Father's. This is emphasized in all four gospels—here in John's, but also at Matthew 19.29, Mark 3.33–35, and Luke 11.27–28

If Jesus' time has not come, and he has refused his mother's implied request, why does he work the miracle? More important, why is it a sign? The gratuitous nature of the act points to some higher meaning than the satisfaction of the bridal party. After all, Jesus turns six huge vessels of water into wine. Since each vessel holds two to three measures, and a measure is about eight gallons, that makes sixteen to twenty-four gallons per vessel—96 to 124 gallons in all! These were not jars meant for wine. They are specifically called *water* vessels, meant to store the vast amounts of water used for ritual purifications. Jesus not only turns that vast quantity of water into wine, but into over a hundred gallons of the highest quality wine, finer than what was first served.

Such abundance is apocalyptic, like the promises of good to come in the New Jerusalem, like a land flowing with milk and honey (Exodus 3.8), like a river flowing with honey (Job 20.17), like bread from heaven (Exodus 16.4), like trees bearing fruit every month (Ezekiel 47.12), like the overflowing cup of Psalm 23.5, like the good returned to those who do good—"ample recompense of crammed-in, sifted-down, overtoppling good showered into your lap" (Luke 6.38). There is a similarity, since this is a Eucharistic sign, to the surplus of loaves and fishes at Matthew 14.20—where over twelve great baskets of food are left over after five thousand have eaten their full.

The sign is also Mosaic, since Moses worked "a sign" (Exodus 7.9) when he turned the water in the Egyptians' great stone jars into blood (7.19). Another sign of the divine largesse occurred when Moses struck a rock in the desert "and water gushed out in abundance," enough to satisfy the whole people's thirst (Numbers 20.11)—a sign Saint Paul applies to Christ as the rock from which Christians drink (1 Corinthians 10.4).

Wine and blood are closely connected in scripture—most obviously in the Eucharist, but in other passages as well. The image of a winepress spilling out blood is used at Isaiah 63.3, Joel 3.13, and Revelation 14.19–20. In all these cases there is abundance of blood—enough to splatter clothes in Isaiah, to overflow a nation in Joel, to foam up to horses' bridles in Revelation. These are visions like that of Marlowe's Faustus: "See, see, where Christ's blood streams in the firmament." The finest wine at Cana, exceeding all need, is a forecast of the precious blood in which people are washed at Revelation 7.14. Christ is addressed as the Lamb, as "using your blood to buy for God men of all tribes and tongues and countries and races" (Revelation 5.9).

The Cana miracle is often used in sermons as an occasion for talking about Christian marriage—though the wedding at Cana was not a Christian but a Jewish one, a point underscored by the presence there of Jewish purification vessels. Despite what has been said at Cana Conferences, the point of this story has nothing really to do with weddings—any more than it has to do with Mary's intercessory powers. Jesus is working a sign that bursts out of the restraints of its occasion, a sign that serves as an induction for his followers into the mysterious journey on the way to his "time."

If one takes the story as showing that Mary can get prayers answered, we are in danger of falling into a false idea of prayer. Saint Augustine says that prayer should not be a kind of magic, in which by making the right approach to God one gets him to do what we want. Our prayer should be that of the Spirit in us, uniting us more closely to God. "When I pray for the recovery of some sick person, my aim is not at all for a magic cure, but that I may submit willingly to whatever you will" (*Confessions* 10.56). We should remember this as we read the gospel passage. Then we may note that Mary makes no request of Jesus. She just states a fact. Then she tells the servants to do whatever Jesus says—as she had submitted herself at the Annunciation: "I attend on the Lord. Let it happen as you say." W. H. Auden had the right view of "petitionary prayer" when he wrote, in the journal *Episcopalian*:

> Our wishes and desires—to pass an exam, to marry the person we love, to sell our house at a good price—are involuntary and therefore not themselves prayers, even if it is God whom we ask to attend to them. They only become prayers in so far as we believe that God knows better than we whether we should be granted or denied what we ask. A petition does not become a prayer unless it ends with the words, spoken or unspoken, "Nevertheless, not as I will, but as thou wilt."

TINTORETTO

The painting shows the six vessels of the story being filled, but the painter clearly did not know how vast they were, with the 120 or so gallons. But he did know that this was a prefiguration of the Eucharist, since he aligns the people in accord with Last Supper iconography. Some other painters seat the bride and groom centrally at the table while Jesus and Mary stand somewhere near, directing the filling of the water vessels. But here Jesus is in the center of a long table with the bridal party on the side away from us, just as in Last Supper paintings. Mary, to his right, takes the position held by Saint John. The bride and groom are moved aside to Jesus' left, with no particular emphasis on them. This is not really their story, but that of the sign. Jesus' gesture with his right hand is almost exactly copied from that in Leonardo's *Last Supper*.

There is also a figure put on the near side of the table with his back to us, in the position often taken by Judas in Last Supper paintings, to jog our associative faculties. But in this scene he is the chief steward, who will taste the wine without knowing where it came from. He is, like Judas, outside the company's social ties, but not culpably so. The wine of Cana is a foretaste of that at the Last Supper. It is what we will drink in the Eucharist. When we understand that, we will see that as Augustine says, "We, too, were water and he made us wine."

3. SERMON ON THE MOUNT

*Seeing the great crowd, he went up the mountain and sat there,
while his disciples gathered about him. Beginning his discourse to
them, he delivered this teaching:*

> *"Happy the poor in spirit,*
> *for theirs is the reign of the heavens.*
> *Happy those in sorrow,*
> *for they shall be consoled.*
> *Happy the gentle,*
> *for the earth is their legacy.*
> *Happy those who hunger and thirst to see right done,*
> *for they shall be satisfied.*
> *Happy the merciful,*
> *for they shall win mercy.*
> *Happy those of clean heart,*
> *for they shall see God.*
> *Happy those making peace,*
> *for they will be known as God's sons.*
> *Happy those persecuted in the cause of right,*
> *for theirs is the reign of the heavens."*

(Matthew 5.1–10)

THE SERMON ON THE MOUNT is a major collection of the teachings of Jesus. It is 107 biblical verses long (Matthew 5.1–7.27), comprising beatitudes, aphorism, parables, authoritative pronouncements, model prayers (including the Our Father). The symbolic purpose of having Jesus go up the mountain is to make this the New Testament version of the delivery of the Law after Moses went up Mount Sinai. The account in Matthew is both less lofty than that in Exodus and more authoritative. In Exodus (19.24), Moses is told to keep the people away, while only he and Aaron approach the holy heights. In Matthew, the people gather around Jesus. Moses is addressed in thunder and lightning and is wrapped in clouds. Jesus sits quietly, the posture of a teacher in antiquity.

Moses passes on the words of God, given to him alone. Jesus speaks on his own authority, contrasting what he says with what had been received before him. A whole section of the sermon (5.21–48) is based on the "You have heard. . . . But I tell you" formula. Six times Jesus contrasts what he teaches with what his followers had learned before him.

"You have heard the prescription 'Eye for eye, tooth for tooth.' But I tell you: Oppose not your attacker. To one who punches your cheek, offer your other cheek." (5.38–39)

Because of the contrasts drawn here between Jesus' teaching and the Mosaic tradition, this section has been called from early days the Antitheses. There is nothing like them anywhere else in the New Testament. This is the most daring break from what was known as the spirit of Moses—it shows why Matthew has Jesus go onto a mountain to forge a new ethos for Christians.

It is an ethos of the world turned upside down, of an inversion of values. The same ethos is contained in Luke's shorter version of this sermon (Luke 6.20–49). Both evangelists are drawing from an earlier collection of Jesus' teachings, and both express the same spirit, making love the center of all actions.

"I say to all who hear me: Love your foes, help those who hate you, praise those who curse, pray for those who abuse you. To one who punches your cheek, offer the other cheek. To one seizing your cloak do not refuse your tunic under it. Whoever asks, give it him. Whoever seizes, do not resist. Exactly how you wish to be treated, in that way treat others. For if you love those who love back, what merit is in that? Sinners themselves love those who love back. If you treat well those treating you well, what merit is in that? That is how sinners act. If you lend only where you calculate a return, what merit is in that? Sinners, too, lend to sinners, calculating an exact return. No, rather love your foes, and treat them well, and lend without any calculation of return. Your great reward will be that you are children of the Highest One, who also favors ingrates and scoundrels. Be just as lenient as your lenient

Father. Be not a judge, then, and you will not be judged. Be no executioner, and you will not be executed. Pardon, and you will be pardoned. Give, and what will be given you is recompense of crammed-in, sifted-down, over toppling good showered into your lap. As you mete out to others, so it will be meted out to you."

(Luke 6.27–38)

These are high and saintly demands, which few if any can claim to fulfill. But what else can truly be called love? Saint Paul made love of just this sort its own measure:

Love is patient, is kind. It does not envy others or brag of itself. It is not swollen with self. It does not embarrass others, nor grasp for everything. It does not flare with anger, nor make excuses for doing wrong. It takes no joy in evil, but delights in truth. It keeps all confidences, all trust, all hope, all pledges. Love will never go out of existence. Prophecy will fail in time, languages too, and knowledge as well. For we know things only partially, or prophesy partially, and when the totality is known, the parts no longer matter. It is like what I spoke as a child, knew as a child, thought as a child, argued as a child—which, now I am grown up, I put off. In the same way we see things in a murky reflection now, but shall see them full-face when what I have known in part I shall know fully, just as I am known. For the present, then, three things matter—believing, hoping, and loving. But supreme is loving.

(1 Corinthians 13.4–13)

There is no way any of us can live up to these high visions of love unless Christ can do it in us, as Paul also said, in a passage that cannot be quoted too often.

Put your mind in Christ's when dealing with one another—for he, having the divine nature from the outset, thinking it no usurpation to be held equal to God, emptied himself out into the nature of a slave.

(Philippians 2.5–7)

TINTORETTO

Tintoretto did not paint a Sermon on the Mount. But it is useful to contemplate again the scene of his finding in the temple, since there too Jesus was preaching out of the depths of the Jewish Law, stressing that the God of Israel is a God of love, that he does not come to cancel the revelation to the people of Israel but to supplement it, as the great prophets had done. His sacrifice of love will emerge out of this teaching on love.

4. TRANSFIGURATION

About a week after he had said these things, he took Peter, John, and James up a mountain to pray. And as he prayed, his face was transfigured and his clothes shone white as lightning. Of a sudden, two men spoke with him, Moses and Elijah, appearing in splendor, to discuss his departure [exodos], *to be accomplished in Jerusalem. Peter and his companions had been deep in sleep; but now they wakened at the sight of his splendor, and that of the men with him. As the two others withdrew, Peter said to Jesus: "Master, how good it is, our being here. Shouldn't we raise three booths, one each for you, for Moses, and for Elijah?" It was spoken in ignorance—for just as he was saying it, a dazzling cloud hovered over them. They felt fear as the two passed into the cloud, and a voice from the cloud said, "This is my Son, my Chosen. Heed him." When this was said, Jesus stood there alone. But they kept their silence, for that time telling no one what they had seen.*

(Luke 9.28–36)

PETER THINKS OF THE BOOTHS (literally, tents) raised in the desert for worship during the Exodus, a thing commemorated in the Jewish Festival of Booths. He is taking up the story of Jewish passage to a new land. The evangelists trace the continuities under the differences between Jesus and his Jewish brothers and sisters. Matthew at the Sermon on the Mount emphasized the contrast between Jesus and Moses. Here and elsewhere, his connections with his forebear are important. Jesus does not go up to the mountain here and invite the crowd to approach him. He singles out three privileged followers—just as Moses was commanded to bring three men, Aaron, Nabab, and Abihu, partway up the mountain with him, after the Law was given, to confirm it (Exodus 24.1).

Jesus' face is transfigured, as Moses' was when he came down from the mountain and "the skin of his face shone because he had been speaking with the Lord" (Exodus 34.29). The lightning of Jesus' appearance and the cloud of glory also resemble the lightning and cloud in which Moses was wrapped (Exodus 24.15–18). These clouds that hover over figures in the gospel are not dimming agencies but dazzling clouds, more like the pillar of fire than any darkening clouds. The connection of

Jesus with Moses is emphasized again when Jesus speaks with him of his own exodus. It continues in Peter's talk of the booths. Since that feast lasted a week, some find a reference to it in the opening words of this episode, "about a week."

The Mosaic importance of this vision is obvious. But why is Elijah there? It is customary to say that Moses and Elijah stand for the two strains in Jewish revelation, the Law and the prophets. But Elijah also had an apocalyptic role. Since he was snatched up to heaven in a fiery chariot (2 Kings 2.11), it was said that he would return at the end of time (Malachi 4.5–6). He was thus a herald of Jesus' own ascent to heaven and his return to judge the world. The conversation of these three indicates a common mission of Jesus and his forebears. But the other two fade into the glory that surrounds Jesus "alone" when the voice speaks of him as Son and Chosen (a messianic title). Peter speaks in ignorance when he treats of the vision as if it contained a kind of human trinity, to be honored equally. The voice of the Father and the hovering cloud make clear what Trinity Jesus belongs to.

Jesus brought his own chosen disciples into this vision to strengthen them for the ordeal they would soon witness, his capture, torture, trial, and death—a thing he had revealed to them enigmatically just before the Transfiguration (Luke 9.22). The fact that the disciples did not prove strong enough to remain with Jesus through his Passion just shows how weak we humans are. But we can look back and remember when Jesus' meaning was revealed to us in the past, and draw comfort from his ultimate vindication as the comrade, heir, and Lord of Moses and Elijah. The vision was later recalled in the Petrine tradition of the New Testament:

We did not rely on tales artfully concocted when we made known to you the power of our Lord Jesus Christ and his return. We saw with these very eyes how he was exalted. As he received honor and glory from God the Father, a voice came to him out of that sublime splendor, "This is my Son, my Chosen, the receiver of my favors. Heed him." We ourselves heard that voice from heaven when we were with him on the holy mountain.

(2 Peter 1.16–18)

During this decade of the rosary we can share the adoration of Peter, be with him on the holy mountain.

TINTORETTO

So far as I know, Tintoretto never painted the transfiguration.

5. LAST SUPPER

As they were eating, he took a loaf of bread, blessed it, broke it, gave it to them, and said, "Take this, it is my body." And taking a cup of wine, he blessed it and gave it to them, and they drank some, all of

them. And he said, "This is my covenantal blood, which is poured out for many. I shall not, I assure you, drink offspring of the vine again till the day when I drink wine new in the reign of God."

(Mark 14.22–25)

MANY THINGS HAPPENED at the Last Supper—Jesus washed his followers' feet, he warned them about what was to happen and predicted their defection, he let Judas know that he was aware of his treachery, he went through the Passover ceremonies. In John's gospel, he delivered a long discourse on love (John's equivalent of the Sermon on the Mount). But for us the most important thing was the institution of the Eucharist, one of the two seminal sacraments. The other one, baptism, occurs only once in anyone's life. But the early Christian agape (love meal) was the source of Christian strength and unity, to be renewed constantly, the mystical body of Christ eating its proper food as our physical bodies do in constant renewal of their fabric.

In this way we fulfill the duty spelled out by Saint Paul in his account of the Last Supper. This is the only gospel story he tells in his letters; it is the earliest account we have of the event—written decades before the gospels were completed; and it is addressed to a particular problem in one community:

What I learned from the Lord I imparted to you—that the Lord Jesus, on the night of his betrayal, took a loaf of bread, blessed it,

*broke it, and said, "This is, for you, my body. Do this to remember
me." After dinner, he did the same with the cup, saying: "This is
a new covenant in my blood. Whenever you drink it, do so to keep
my memory."*

*Whenever, therefore, you eat of this bread or drink from this
cup, you herald the Lord's death, until his coming. And whoever
eats this bread or drinks from the Lord's cup disgracefully bears
guilt for the Lord's body and blood. Only after qualifying oneself
should one eat of the bread or drink from the cup. The one who
eats and drinks, without acknowledging the body, is eating and
drinking a sentence [krima] on himself.*

(1 Corinthians 11.23–29)

The problem in the community that Paul was addressing
was the profanation of the meal of unity by selfish factions
hoarding food and drink to themselves:

*When you gather it is not to eat the Lord's supper. Rather, the in-
dividual grabs food to eat beforehand, leaving some to go hungry
and others to get drunk. Do you not have your own homes for [pri-
vate] eating and drinking? Or do you mean to insult the gathering of the Lord, and show contempt for those who lack food? . . .
Therefore, brothers, wait for others to eat with you. If you are too
hungry for that, eat beforehand in your home, so that in the gathering you do not serve a sentence [krima] on yourself.*

(1 Corinthians 11.20–22, 33–34)

The way one "qualifies oneself" to eat the agape meal is to "acknowledge the body" of all the faithful as the mystical body
of Christ, not sequestering food or drink to oneself or to a
faction.

The cup of blessing, once blessed, is it not a participation in the blood of Christ? The bread we break, is it not a participation in the body of Christ? We many are one bread, one body, because we all partake of a single bread.

(1 Corinthians 10.16–17)

This is the passage from which Augustine took his Eucharistic theology. In Sermon 272 he said:

If you want to know what is the body of Christ, hear what the Apostle [Paul] tells believers: "You are Christ's body and his members." If, then, you are Christ's body and his members, it is our symbol that lies on the Lord's altar—what you receive is a symbol of yourself. When you say "Amen" to what you are, your saying it affirms it. You hear "The Body of Christ," and you answer "Amen," and you must *be* the body of Christ to make that "Amen" take effect. And why are you a bread? Hear the Apostle again, speaking of this very symbol: "We many are one bread, one body."

In Sermon 272, he told newly baptized Christians what the Eucharist means to them:

This bread makes clear how you should love your union with one another. Could the bread have been made from one grain, or were many grains of wheat required? Yet before they cohered as bread, each grain was isolated. They were fused in water, after being ground together. Unless wheat is pounded, and then moistened with water, it can hardly take on the new identity we call bread. In the same way, you had to be ground by the ordeal of fasting and exorcism in preparation of baptism's waters, and in this way you were watered in order to take on the new identity of bread. But bread must be finished by baking in fire. In this way you were being ground and pounded, as it were, by the humiliation of fasting and the mystery of exorcism. After that, the water of baptism moistened you into bread. But the dough does not become bread until it is baked in fire. And what does fire represent for you? It is the anointing with oil. Oil, which feeds fire, is the symbol of the Holy Spirit . . . the Holy Spirit comes to you, fire after water, and you are baked into the bread which is Christ's body. That is how your unity is symbolized.

At the Mass, the sacred meal confirms us in our unity as the body of Christ. At communion, says Augustine, we receive what we are. The power of the divine Word to unite us is a completion of the wonder that belongs even to human words. Augustine often called the breaking of the bread at Mass the breaking open of the meaning of words in the sacred texts. And he told his hearers how this mystery operates:

The words I am uttering penetrate your senses, so that every hearer holds them, yet withholds them from no other. Not held, the words could not inform. Withheld, no other could share them. Though my talk is, admittedly, broken up into words and syllables, yet you do not take in this portion or that, as when picking at your food. All of you hear all of it, though each takes all individually. I have no worry that, by giving all to one, the others are deprived. I hope, instead, that everyone will consume everything; so that, denying no other ear or mind, you take all to yourselves, yet leave all to all others. Nor is this done temporally, by turns—my words first going to one, who must pass it on to another. But for individual failures of memory, everyone who came to hear what I say can take it all off, each on one's separate way.

TINTORETTO

Paul says that at Mass we "herald Christ's death." The blood offered the followers at the Last Supper was "poured out," making the meal and the death a mystical unity. This is brilliantly presented by Tintoretto when he makes Jesus stretch out his arms, in giving the broken bits of bread, as they will be stretched on the Cross. He leans forward eagerly, suggesting the way he will accept death to complete the Father's plan. The whole mystery of the Eucharist could not be more economically presented—not even in Chesterton's wonderful answer, given by King Alfred to Danish mockers of his Christian band.

> Oh, truly we be broken hearts,
> For that cause, it is said,
> We light our candles to the Lord,
> Who broke himself for bread.

IV. The Sorrowful Mysteries

MOST BIBLE SCHOLARS THINK the Passion narratives are the oldest parts of the gospels. This is the defining sequence of the Christian proclamation. All the other parts of it are created to supplement, explain, and emphasize these tragic events. The contemplation of these mysteries is both hard and easy—hard in the sense that they are painful to think of, but easy in that most Christians have many indelible images of the events, derived from Lenten exercises, sermons, retreats, and artworks (including movies). They are seared on our brains.

1. AGONY IN THE GARDEN

They arrive at a place known as Gethsemane, and he says to his fol-lowers, "Stay here while I pray." And he takes Peter, James, and John with him. But as he began to feel terrified and helpless, he tells them, "I am anguished enough to die. Stay here and keep alert." Go-ing a little farther, he fell on the ground and prayed that, if it were possible, his time might go away. He said: "Abba, Father, you can do all things—yet your will, not mine, prevail."

He comes back and finds them asleep, and says to Peter: "Sleep you, Simon? Not one hour could you stay awake? Keep awake, and pray that you enter not into the Trial [Peirasmos]. *The spirit is ready, but the flesh fails." Going off again, he prayed. And coming back again, he found them asleep, since their eyes were heavy, and they could not give an account of themselves.*

A third time he returns and says, "Still asleep, still unwatchful? Let be. The time is come. The Son of Man is given over to the hands of sinners. Get up and come, my betrayer has arrived."

(Mark 14.32–42)

As at the Sermon on the Mount or the Transfiguration, Jesus goes up a mountain for this spiritual experience—in this case, the steep rise of the Mount of Olives, over against what we know as the Old City. As at the Transfiguration, he takes his chosen three followers halfway up the mountain. And once again they fall asleep as he wrestles with his destiny—and theirs—above their heads. This is an apocalyptic episode, a forecast of the final struggle between good and evil. It has many overtones of the apocalyptic prayer that introduces this (and every) decade of beads, the Our Father. As in the prayer, Jesus asks that God's will be done. He asks, as well, that his followers escape the wrenching final Trial *(Peirasmos)* that we pray to avoid in the Our Father. He warns the followers to be on the watch—which is his warning about expectation of the end-time, which will also come upon sleeping humans like a thief in the night (1 Thessalonians 5.2; Matthew 24.43). The duty of perpetual wakefulness underlies parables like that of the wise and foolish virgins, or the unattended wedding.

The cup Jesus asks not to drain recalls the cups of wrath in Jewish scripture (Isaiah 51.17, for instance) and the phials of curses poured out in Revelation. It is the cup he had fore-

Annunciation

Visitation

Nativity with Adoration of Shepherds

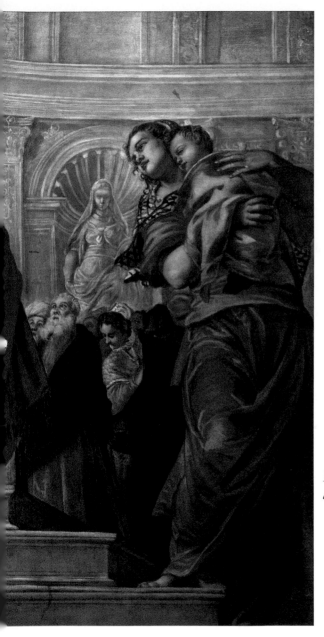

*Presentation of Christ
at the Temple*

*Christ Among the
Scholars of the Law*

Baptism of Christ

*The Wedding
Feast at Cana*

Last Supper

Agony in the Garden

The Flagellation of Christ

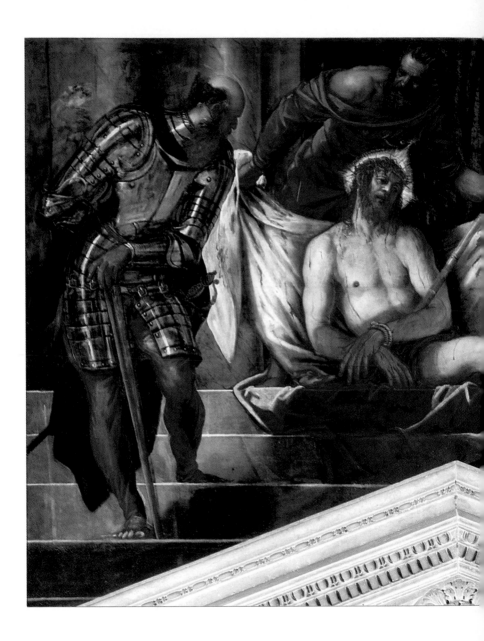

Ecce Homo
(Crowning
with
Thorns)

Christ on the Way to Calvary

Crucifixion

Resurrection of Christ

OPPOSITE: *Ascension of Christ*

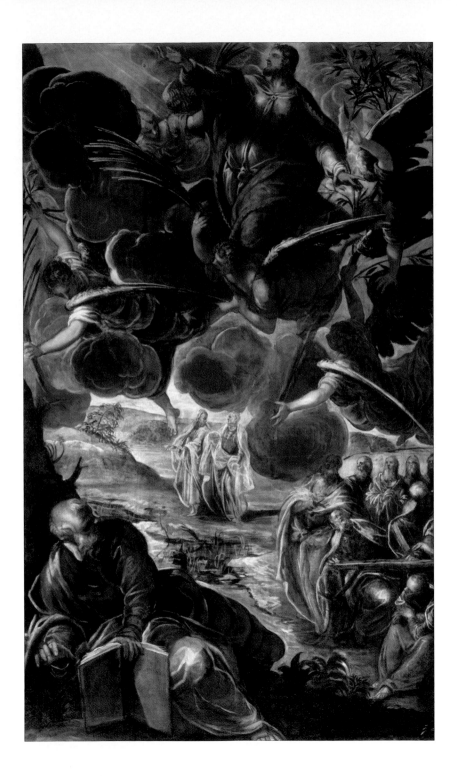

Assumption of the Virgin

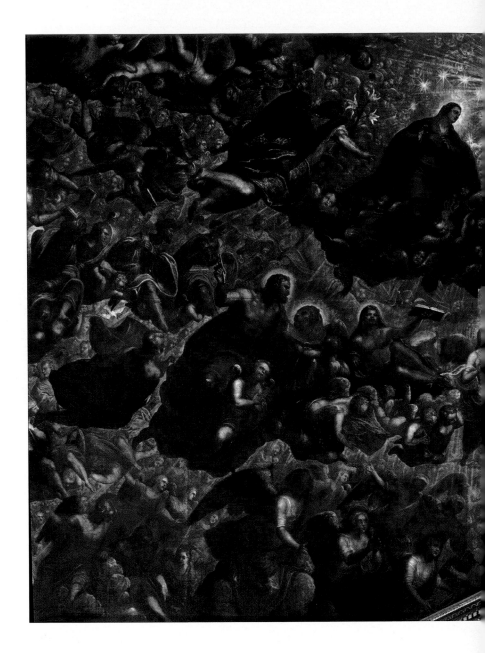

Paradise

seen as part of his Passion: "Can you drink the cup I drink, be baptized with the baptism that will baptize me?" (Mark 10.38). Jesus' sweating of blood is a prodigy of the eschatological struggle—like the rent veil, earthquake, and eclipse of his crucifixion. Jesus is fighting the showdown fight ahead of time, for all of us.

Jesus is near to death in spirit before his tortures even begin. That would be understandable for us ordinary humans. Our fear of death, our sense of its unfairness, our protest against such torment, our regrets and guilt, our longing for earthly delights being taken away from us—all those emotions would crowd in on us, so we could not even distinguish one from the other in their jostling urgencies. But something loftier and deeper is being described here. Christ is facing the ultimate enemy of mankind, and taking on the burden of all the sins to be purged away in his person. He is bringing victory by a path that goes through, not his guilt and regrets, but all those he is redeeming. John Henry Newman found in this the source of his anguish, enough to rend the human frame and make it shed a blood of pure mental anguish. Newman's sermon is called "The Mental Sufferings of Our Lord in His Passion."

It is the long history of a world, and God alone can bear the load of it. Hopes blighted, vows broken, lights quenched, warnings scorned, opportunities lost, the innocent betrayed, the young hardened, the penitent relapsing, the just overcome, the aged failing, the sophistry of misbelief, the willfulness of passion, the obduracy of pride, the tyranny of habit, the canker of remorse, the wasting fever of care, the anguish of shame, the pining of disappointment, the sickness of despair; such cruel, such pitiable spectacles, such heart-rending, revolting, detestable, maddening scenes; nay, the haggard faces, the convulsed lips, the flushed cheek, the dark brow of the willing victims of rebellion, they are all before him now; they are upon him and in him.

Newman's passage on the Agony I had for decades considered the most moving one possible. But then I read a letter Hilaire Belloc wrote a friend from the Holy Land, just after he had gone to the Mount of Olives (Olivet):

The Agony in the Garden is the core and height of the Passion. The near anticipation of a dreadful thing is the acme of its effect: when the falling of a blow is morally certain, the last awaiting of it is the master trial. The sequel is more exhausted; and that is why all those who know the significance of Christendom should revere—even beyond the rock of the Cross of the Holy Sepulchre itself, or the Altar of the Assumption in Nazareth or the Grotto of Bethlehem— Olivet. *"Dieu même a craint la Mort."* [Fear of death even God experienced.] That is great poetry and therefore, justly interpreted, sound truth: sound theology. Not that God himself can suffer, but that God was so intensely, so intimately man in the Incarnation that the memories and experience of divinity and humanity are united therein: and through it, the worst pain of the creature is *known*, by actual experience of our own kind, by the Creator. . . . [Death] is a curtain of iron, a gulf impassable, an impenetrable darkness, and a distance as it were limitless, infinite. The miracle whereby such an enormity coming upon immortal souls does not breed despair, is the chief miracle of the Incarnation—and to work that miracle, the Incarnate—with what supreme energy—accepted our pain, almost refused it, but accepted it, and it was greater than any pain of ours, physically beyond endurance and in the spirit a descent into hell.

Belloc's latest biographer, A. N. Wilson, says of that passage all that needs saying: "It is worth quoting this letter so fully, because there is so much Belloc here, and so much of him which he normally kept carefully concealed. It shows more nakedly than anything he ever wrote, how close the very thought of death brought him to despair; and how the one thing that could rescue him from despair was the Passion of his Savior." That is probably true of many Christians, whose pain is relieved by the pain of Jesus.

TINTORETTO

Tintoretto's painting of the Agony defies spatial relationships to create three different realities. To the left, coming through what Virgil called "the taciturnities of a tactful moon," the arresting party is carefully groping its way. In the group on the lower right, Peter's bald pate catches the mild moonlight, as he stirs at the sound of the clattering troop, though the sleeping John has a bright light shed on him from the supernatural glow above him. In that higher section of the picture, chromatic spheres of a weird unearthly sort prevail, a sinister rainbow of doom, as the angel brings the cup that Jesus must drain. Jesus himself turns from the cup, and would seem at first glance to be defying his own advice to keep alert. I believe Jesus is having a kind of waking dream, the cup that is mere metaphor in the gospel texts being thrust insistently at him. He turns away, instinctively resisting, though his resolve to do the Father's will is what makes the scene so moving. Tintoretto painted Moses in such a realm of higher light, while the people of Israel pursued their blind concerns below. Jesus is always just above and beyond his followers, working out their salvation in ways they cannot understand.

(There was a special meaning in this work for Tintoretto's fellow Venetians. The feast of Holy Thursday, the time of the Agony in the Garden, was marked by the Venetian ruler, the doge, when he donned the *corrucio*, a blood red cassock, a symbol of the precious blood of Jesus shed here before the tortures began. One of the city's most revered relics was a bit of that blood from the garden. Tintoretto puts the *corrucio* on Jesus here. Few painters have found a convincing or dignified way to show Jesus actually sweating blood. Tintoretto achieves the effect of that by putting the blood garment on him, and arranging the strange coruscations of color so that the picture, in effect, bleeds from its vivid and lurid upper right-hand portion.)

2. SCOURGING

So Pilate, eager to pacify the mob, released to it Barabbas and sentenced Jesus, after scourging, to be crucified.

(Mark 15.15)

ALL THREE EVANGELISTS who report the scourging do so in only one word—"after scourging" here is just a participle in the Greek, "having scourged." Luke omits this torture from his account of the Passion, though he, like Mark and Matthew, reports Jesus' prediction that he would be scourged. It was thus an integral part of the Passion.

> *As they made their way to Jerusalem, with Jesus in the lead, his followers were shocked, and those trailing behind were in the grip of fear. Again taking the Twelve aside, he began to say what was about to happen to him: "We go now to Jerusalem, where the Son of Man will be turned over to the chief priests and scribes, who will sentence him to death and turn him over to the Romans, who will mock him, spit on him, scourge him, and kill him. But on the third day he will rise."*
> (Mark 10.32–34 [= Matthew 20.18–19; Luke 18.31–33])

In general, the evangelists do not go into physical details of Christ's suffering—for example, whether the crown of thorns pierced his skin, or just what was entailed in going to the place of execution, or how he was fastened to the cross (no mention is made of nails in the Passion narratives). The scourging is mentioned almost as an aside because it was part of the penalty of crucifixion. The condemned man was scourged while bound to a low post or higher pillar in order to weaken him. That way he could put up less resistance to those who must fix him on the cross.

Though the active Greek participle may suggest that Pilate himself oversaw the flagellation, it was probably left to the discretion of the executioners how far to break the condemned man's resistance. It seems likely that the unrepentant criminal crucified with Jesus would have been whipped strenuously before bringing him to execution. The soldiers were not to kill their prisoner or make him unconscious before the punishment to which this was just a prelude, and all three victims at this execution will be able to speak from the cross.

Since Jesus had submitted to the whole arrest-and-trial procedure, there was little need to subdue him—and not all the soldiers were sadists, as the later words of the centurion show (Mark 15.39). Nonetheless, the scourging of Jesus must have been severe. That alone seems to explain his inability to carry the cross, a normal part of the execution process. It would also explain why he died earlier than Pilate expected (Mark 15.44–45). The mocking of Jesus in his "coronation" points to gratuitous cruelty in his treatment. Christ would be spared no pain, ordeal, indignity, or humiliation. Christian martyrs would summon their resolve with the thought that nothing inflicted on them could surpass what Jesus underwent for their sake. We ordinary Christians have the same consolation.

TINTORETTO

Jesus sags from the pillar in that bowed-down posture he was given in the scene of his baptism, as if assuming all the load of sin, a Christian Atlas carrying the world on his shoulders. Tintoretto is able to suggest the power of Jesus even as he is passive under the lash. This is a chosen punishment, an achievement. The brute, faceless, muscular torturer is as lacking in spirit as his brandished lash. Jesus' face, too, is hidden, but intelligence radiates through his body. The clash of mind versus matter has seldom been so strikingly portrayed.

3. CROWNING WITH THORNS

*The soldiers then [after the scourging] took him inside the courtyard,
known as the pretorium, and summoned their whole cohort. They
clothed him in purple. Weaving a wreath* [stephanos] *of thorns, they
placed that on him. Then they began to acclaim him,* "Hail, the
Jews' king!" *And they hit him in the head with a stick and spat on
him, and fell to their knees to pay him homage. After having had
this fun with him* [enepaixan], *they stripped away the purple and
put his own clothes back on him.*

(Mark 15.16–20)

RAYMOND BROWN SAYS that Luke has a more plausible place-ment of this episode—during the time when Jesus was still in the hands of the temple police. He says it seems unlikely that the Roman soldiers, deputed as a team of executioners, would interrupt their assignment, of which scourging was the first step, to take time for summoning their whole cohort at the pretorium, "having fun" with the condemned man, dressing him up, and then redressing him—especially since they had to hurry to complete the execution before the Sabbath, so as not to alienate their Jewish subjects. On the other hand, Brown thinks that mockery of Christ as a would-be king (as opposed to would-be prophet) is more likely to come from Roman lips—and such mockery is placed on them by Luke (23.37) during the crucifixion itself.

In any case, the wreath *(stephanos)* of thorns is part of the pregospel tradition. Later Christians would make this wreath a crown that was a torture device, puncturing the scalp. But "crowns" at the time were diadems (used in other mock coro-nations) or wreaths (like the laurel wreaths worn by Roman emperors). The wreath, like the purple robe, is an instrument of mockery, not torture. Later iconography would show Jesus bleeding from the wreath, but the earliest known depictions of the crucifixion do not.

There is also a problem in rapidly finding at hand near the pretorium any Palestinian thorns that could conceivably be "woven" together. Brown refers to "the practical realization that stiff thorns cannot be woven, even if the branches can be entangled"—and the latter could not be made a "wreath." He thinks the term "thorn" *(akantha)* might be used loosely to cover the acanthus plant *(akanthos)*, used for decorative circlets (as on the Corinthian capitals of ancient architecture). What is needed is a "royal" wreath to go with the royal purple, for the purposes of faked monarchy. The point is that the wreath should be a mock laurel.

Here we get a supreme expression of the cruel paradox that runs through the whole Passion narrative, that men are sitting in judgment on their own Judge, ruling over their Ruler, torturing their Healer, damning their Savior. The soldiers, after decking Jesus out in tawdry finery to suggest he is an exalted human, shower him with blows and spit to prove that he is less than human—and all the while he is *more* than human. The First is truly made last, brought as low as can be, made the sport of idle and thoughtless people as well as jealous priests and irresponsible rulers. The condemnation of Jesus, who will save mankind, is made the joint act of all mankind. That is what makes the attempt to blame Christ's death on the Jews not merely unjust but pointless. At the Nativity, high and low (Magi and shepherds) secretly united to receive the Savior. Here, high and low publicly unite against him. Chesterton, as usual, got the point of the gospel narratives. As he put it in *The Everlasting Man*:

The mob went along with the Sadducees and the Pharisees, the philosophers and the moralists. It went along with the imperial magistrates and the sacred priests, the scribes and the soldiers, that the one universal human spirit might suffer a universal condemnation; that there might be one deep, unanimous chorus of approval and harmony when Man was rejected of men.

The mock wreath was probably put aside, along with the mock robe, when the "funning" ended. A wreath or diadem would not have stayed on Christ while blows rained on him, or while he fell on the way to the cross, or during the even more agonizing process of putting Jesus on the cross. When the wreath was removed, Jesus' clothes were put back on him. Though the condemned man usually carried his cross while nude, Jesus' clothes are put back on—they need to be there for the soldiers to cast lots for them at Calvary, fulfilling a prophecy.

TINTORETTO

Tintoretto's painting of the crowning with thorns is in a private collection. But the results of the mocking are clear in his painting of the "Ecce Homo," that scene where Pilate shows Jesus to the mob and says, "Behold the man" (John 19.5). Jesus is normally shown in this episode standing beside Pilate. Tintoretto shows him prostrate, fresh from his mocking. He is not only crowned with thorns. He bears the mock scepter given him. The "kingly" robe put on him is open behind him to show that it is blood drenched. He sprawls on a red cloth, and red runs through the clothing of Pilate and the soldiers. It is reflected in the soldier's armor. We see the whole scene as through a mist of blood, the blood of which the four Roman figures surrounding Christ are guilty.

4. CARRYING THE CROSS

When they led him out, they took hold of a certain Simon from Cyrene, who was coming in from the field, and made him carry the cross behind Jesus. Along the way there was an exceedingly large crowd of people, along with some women who beat their breasts and lamented. But Jesus turned to them and said, "Daughters of Jerusalem, wail not for me but for yourselves and for your children. A time is at hand when it will be said, 'Blessed the barren, the wombs that bore not, the breasts that nursed not.' They will start to tell the mountains, 'Collapse on us' and the hills, 'Blanket us.' For if they do this to wood that is green, what will happen to the dry wood?" Two others were being led off with him, both of them criminals to be executed.

(Luke 23.26–32)

FOR CATHOLICS OF MY GENERATION, this mystery has many and complex associations—too many, if one is interested in contemplation of the gospel account. For these associations do not come from the gospels but from the pious practice, performed privately or by the community, called the Stations of the Cross. These "stops" (stations) were marked originally by attempts, in Jerusalem, to follow the steps of Jesus on his way from the judgment seat to Calvary. The Franciscans, who had charge of the holy places from the fourteenth century on, encouraged this effort to retrace Jesus' route. The path finally settled on, after many experiments, is still called the Via Dolorosa (Path of Sadness). It is followed by processions and pilgrims, especially on Good Friday or in Lent. Smaller replicas of the Path were built in monasteries or gardens outside the Holy Land, with little chapels or monuments to mark each of the stations. Eventually, an abbreviated form of it was created in cloister walks or along the side walls of churches, each stop marked by a painted or sculpted image of what happened there.

The number of stops was originally spun out at length, to make the pilgrimage more intense and complete—there were as many as thirty-seven "stations" observed in Jerusalem. We have seen that the same proliferation of mysteries could be found in the early forms of the rosary. As with that devotion, however, the number was trimmed and made more stable over time, finally being fixed at fourteen. This process was not completed until the eighteenth century, when the devotion became intensely popular, encouraged by preachers of its efficacy like the Franciscan Saint Leonard of Port Maurice. That is when indulgences were widely granted to the performance of the fourteen stations. Originally, the indulgences had been given only to Franciscans, as guardians of the Via. The Stations of the Cross were as closely associated with the Franciscans as the rosary with the Dominicans. Soon the indulgences were granted to Franciscan allies *(tertiaries)*, later to those following the stations in places especially blessed for that purpose, and finally to anyone "making the stations" along his or her parish church walls. The old *Catholic Encylopedia* observed: "It may be safely asserted that there is no devotion more richly endowed with indulgences than the Way of the Cross." The same problem arose from that as from indulgences given to recitation of the rosary—namely, a rapid and rote performance to get the reward.

The canonical fourteen stops are these:

1. Pilate sentences Jesus.
2. Jesus takes up the cross.
3. Jesus falls the first time.
4. Jesus meets Mary.
5. Simon from Cyrene is made to help carry the cross.
6. Veronica wipes Jesus' face with her veil.
7. Jesus falls the second time.
8. Jesus speaks to the daughters of Jerusalem.
9. Jesus falls the third time.

10. Arrived at Calvary, Jesus is given gall to drink.
11. Jesus is nailed to the cross.
12. Jesus dies on the cross.
13. Jesus is taken down from the cross.
14. Jesus is laid in his tomb.

The only things in this list that come from the gospels are 1, 8, and 12–13. The other nine stops are based on legend—the three falls, the meeting with Mary, Veronica's veil, and so forth. It might be thought that number 5 comes from the gospels—it partly, misleadingly, does. What is shown at that station is Simon somehow helping Jesus to carry the cross. But all three synoptic gospels have Simon alone carrying the cross from the outset. The fourth gospel, John's, does not mention Simon.

One can meditate on whichever aspects of the Sorrowful Way one finds most meaningful. But for those who want to stick to the gospels, it helps to know what is established there. Simon would not have carried the whole cross, both the upright post and the crossbar. A cross substantial enough to be planted deep and to sustain a man's weight would be very heavy and ungainly. The upright, therefore, was already planted at the place of execution, where it could be used over and over. Roman sources confirm that the man sentenced to be crucified carried only his own crossbar, loaded on his shoulders with his arms looped over it and tied. Even that would be a taxing burden, especially if the distance was very great. (It is great along the current Via Dolorosa, but archaeologists now deny that this could have been the actual route.) The legendary three falls were inserted because it was thought that Jesus was carrying the whole cross. In the stations, Simon is brought in only after the first fall, and he can only help rather than relieve Jesus entirely, or the second and third falls will be unmotivated.

Why did Jesus not carry his own cross? The conscripting of another man, innocent of any crime, to perform this part of his sentence could not have been a privilege accorded Jesus. Most now suppose that the scourging had so weakened him that he could not stay upright with the crossbar on his shoulders. Mark's gospel, the earliest, not only identifies Simon but two of his sons (Alexander and Rufus), which leads scholars to think that Simon is a historical figure, whose sons would have been known to the early Christian community—which means that his experience made him and his family become Christians. This suggests that Simon was the first to make the *real* Stations of the Cross, to the good of his soul.

When Jesus speaks to the women and predicts a great terror coming, what event is he referring to? The destruction of the temple? Future persecution of Christians? Or the great Trial *(Peirasmos)* at the end of time? This seems most likely, since Jesus has just told the three disciples in the garden to pray that they not suffer the *Peirasmos* (Matthew 26.41). That is also the prayer he voices for the church in the Our Father (Matthew 6.13). Besides, if the destruction of the temple were being predicted, the "they" who do things to the dry wood would be Romans. And Jesus told the disciples at the Last Supper, "The Prince of This World is near" (John 14.30). The context of the agony is eschatological, Christ battling the cosmic powers of darkness as a foretaste of the final showdown.

He describes his suffering as done to "green wood." Undried wood is the hardest to kindle, usually set aside to be used last, after it has aged. But "they" have a heat that can devour even the young wood—thus, a fortiori, even more fiercely the

dry wood (the suffering humanity that will face the apoca-
lypse). When Jesus stops to comfort the women (Mary is not
mentioned among them), he is thinking of others, even in his
own time of pain. He turns to the people for whom he is dying.
His mystical body will suffer in the future, and can take comfort in the thought that it was with him, it was on his mind, at
this literally excruciating moment. The words searingly im-
printed by the gospel account of the Via Crucis are "Wail not
for me, but for yourselves."

TINTORETTO

Practically no painter of this sequence shows what the Roman
descriptions establish—that the condemned man bore the crossbar bound on his shoulders. And none show Simon carrying
that crossbar behind Jesus. The iconography of the subject
came from the hundreds of depictions of it as part of the Stations of the Cross. That is, it shows Jesus at first carrying the
whole cross himself, and then Simon doing something to help
him. The help is never convincingly shown. If Simon takes up
part of the crossbar, the weight of the upright is just thrown
more onto Jesus. If he picks up the end of the upright, the
same shift occurs. Tintoretto does not even try to make the
help really functional. Simon (who is modeled on Tintoretto's
patron, a grandee of the confraternity for which this scene was
painted) just stands above one arm of the crossbar giving moral
support.

But Tintoretto always has some theological reflection to
add to the customary image. The Confraternity of Saint Roch
had religious floats in the Venetian processions on holy days
like that of Corpus Domini, where the tableau of Christ on the

way to the cross would be seen from below, as in this picture. The long train winds up a hill, and the soldier with the Roman flag on the right treats it as a triumphal march. In fact, it *is* a paradoxical triumphal march. The commanding figure of Jesus is on the way to a battle he wins. The lurid sky is full of portent, of menace, but threatening in truth the ones who think they are conquering. The two criminals being dragged and pushed below are in the shadow; but Christ is haloed with a mysterious light that means all worldly judgments are themselves under judgment, and he will conquer from the cross.

5. CRUCIFIXION

And they bring him to a place, Golgotha, which is in translation the Skull Place. And they were trying to give him drugged wine, but he did not accept it. And they crucify him, and they separate his clothes, casting lots to see who will get what. It was the third hour [noon] when they crucified him. An inscription identified the charge: "King of the Jews." Along with him they crucify two bandits, one on his right, one on his left.

(Mark 15.22–27)

One of the criminals suspended there was taunting him: "Aren't you the Messiah? Save yourself—and us." But the other responded, rebuking him: "Have you no fear of God? You are sentenced as he is, and we are getting what our crimes deserve, while this man has done no wrong." And he addressed Jesus: "Remember me when you enter on your reign." Jesus told him: "This day, with me, you will be in Paradise."

(Luke 23.39–43)

By the cross of Jesus stood his mother, and his mother's sister, Mary the wife of Clopas, and Mary Magdalene. Jesus saw his mother standing with his beloved disciple, and he said to his mother: "Woman, here is your son." And to the disciple: "Here is your mother." From that moment the disciple took her into his care.

(John 19.25–27)

There was darkness over all the earth, beginning at the sixth hour and lasting till the ninth. And at the ninth hour Jesus shouted in a loud voice, "Eloi, Eloi, lama sabachthani?"—in translation, "My God, my God, why have you abandoned me?" Some standing near, hearing this, said, "That is Elijah he is calling to." One man, running off to soak a sponge with harsh wine, put it on a reed, and was trying to give him drink, saying: "Wait! See if Elijah comes to take him down." But Jesus, having lifted a loud cry, ceased to breathe. And the temple curtain was ripped apart from top to bottom. When the centurion standing before him saw how he died, he said, "This man was in fact the Son of God."

(Mark 15.33–39)

Since it was the eve of the Passover, and the bodies should not be hanging still on the Sabbath, and this was a special Sabbath day, the Jews requested Pilate to break the men's legs and take them down. So the soldiers came and broke the first man's legs, and then those of the one crucified with him. But when they came to Jesus, they saw he was already dead, and did not break his legs. One of the soldiers, rather, pierced his side with a spear, and blood and water ran out suddenly. An eyewitness has averred this, and his witness is a true one you can believe. This occurred to fulfill the scripture "You shall not break a bone of him." And there is another scripture: "They shall look upon the one they stabbed."

(John 19.31–37)

I HAVE GIVEN only some of the details from the crucifixion scene. The Passion story, as the original core of the gospels, is told in some detail—which makes it all the more surprising that Jesus' sufferings are not directly mentioned. The act of fixing him on the cross, raising him, securing him, is covered by all four evangelists in one word: *staurousin* ("they crucify"). It is not even said which of the two modes of fixing a man to the cross was used—by ropes or by nails. The fact that nails were used comes out only indirectly—in the account, after the Resurrection, of Thomas's challenge: "Unless I can see the proof of the nails in his hands, unless I put my finger into the holes left by the nails, and my hand into his side, I shall never believe" (John 20.25).

It is sometimes supposed by modern readers that the use of nails was the crueler punishment, but that is not necessarily so. The nails were not hammered into the palms of the hand— there is no bone structure there that would support a whole body's weight, so the nails would just slip out between the fingers. The nails were put through the bony cage of the wrist. But that could sever the artery, as in suicide by slitting one's wrists, and make the condemned man die faster. The real torture of the cross involved long survival under immense pain. The hanging body would constrict breathing, making the person pull himself up on aching muscles to catch his breath. This could go on for hours, even for days. In the case of Jesus, however, Pilate is surprised to hear that he dies so soon (Mark 15.44–45). This may have been the result not only of the scourging but of bleeding through the wrists.

Jesus is always depicted in art with nails through his palms, the result of preaching that applied Psalm 22.17 to Jesus. In the Septuagint Greek translation of that psalm (but not in the original Hebrew) the verse reads: "They have dug holes in my hands and feet." Scholars argue that this verse was not in the minds of the evangelists themselves—otherwise they would have cited it explicitly, as they do other prophecies of the Passion.

To me the most comforting words in scripture are those spoken when Jesus turns to a sinner, our comrade and brother, and pronounces a happy doom: "This day, with me, you will be in Paradise." Chesterton has a poem in which the hope of sinners is expressed—the hope of the weak, the strayed,

> And many a thief with thankful eyes
> Like his who climbed the torturing tree,
> And drank that night in Paradise.

Jesus thinks of others, even from the cross, and speaks the only loving words he is recorded in the gospels as addressing to Mary: "Mother, this is your son." Though he is leaving her, he puts her under the protection of his beloved disciple. Pious commentators have claimed that John is to be protected by her. But John takes her into his care. Augustine finds Mary now integrated into the Christian community, after being excluded from Jesus' public ministry. In *Interpreting John's Gospel* (119.1), he writes:

Then [at Cana] he was about to work a miracle, so he put aside as unknown the mother, not of his divinity, but of his weakness. Now, however, suffering the human fate, he extends a human affection to the source of his humanity. Then, Mary's creator made known his power. Now, however, Mary's human offspring was hanging on a cross.

Raymond Brown points out that in giving her into the care of John, Jesus makes John the custodian of the whole tradition of his life, giving authority to the gospel issued in John's name (John 19.35). At Cana, Mary was treated only as a member of Jesus' physical family. Now she is part of the family of the disciples, the new spiritual entity, the church:

[Christ's saying] brings the natural family (Jesus' mother) into the relationship of discipleship by making her the mother of the beloved disciple who takes her into his own realm of discipleship. The woman whose intervention at Cana on behalf of earthly needs was rejected because the hour had not yet come is now given a role in the realm engendered from above after the hour has come.

During this decade of the rosary we stand at the cross with Mary and John, our sister and brother in the faith, in a solidarity of faith and life created by the sacrifice we forever look on.

About Jesus' cry of abandonment, which is a quotation of Psalm 22.1, there is an ultimate mystery. Raymond Brown takes it in conjunction with the apocalyptic signs—the rent temple curtain, the darkness and earthquake—as a voice spoken from the cosmic struggle foreshadowed here, the dread *Peirasmos* that Jesus has prayed for his followers to be spared. It is the rending of the whole cosmos finding expression. It should be remembered that Jesus is quoting the opening words of a psalm that works itself toward hope in the following verses. The very fact that he is praying to God is an expression of hope in the midst of anguish, and a comfort to those who resist despair. Nonetheless, these are words of such awful import that Chesterton could say (in *The Everlasting Man*) that they go beyond our powers to comprehend:

> We may surely be silent about the end and the extremity; when a cry was driven out of that darkness in words dreadfully distinct and dreadfully unintelligible, which man shall never understand in all the eternity they have purchased for him; and for an annihilating instant an abyss that is not for our thoughts had opened even in the unity of the absolute; and God had been forsaken of God.

TINTORETTO

Tintoretto's great painting of the crucifixion fills a wall forty feet wide in the boardroom of the Confraternity of Saint Roch. It develops an idea that is present in many crucifixion paintings of the time—that Jesus on the cross is like Jesus judging all history at the end of time. The disposition of people is therefore like that of the saved and damned in *Last Judgments*—the saved on Jesus' right (our left), the damned on his left. The connection between the two events was shown, in *Last Judgments*, by a display of the instruments of the Passion (cross, nails, crown of thorns, spear) around the Judge. This meant that he got his authority to judge by virtue of the sufferings he underwent for the saved.

The picture shows a crowd forming a circle around the cross. We, standing at the break in the circle, complete it as part of the group around the collapsed Virgin. On the "saved" side of the picture is Jerusalem, with a prophet pointing to Jesus. The good centurion is on a white horse, while his surrogate offers the wine-soaked sponge to Jesus. The cross with the good thief is being raised in its socket as the man turns with hope to Jesus—like the souls being drawn up by the rosary in Michelangelo's *Last Judgment*. On Jesus' left are the Jewish priests, the soldiers gambling for Christ's clothes, and the bad thief wrestling against attempts to fix him on his cross.

To show Jesus as the timeless judge as well as the temporal victim, Tintoretto makes him *preside* on the cross. He is only partly in time. His arms stretch along the upper edge of the painting almost as if he were going to take flight. The large halo around him is only a semicircle, with a tarnished glow. If the upper semicircle were shown, it would be resplendent in heaven. Since Jesus' arms stretch along the upper limit of the picture, the projection of the cross above his head, where the inscription is normally nailed, is missing. To displace Jesus from his temporal abode, the cross itself is ambiguously located in the fictional space. At the upper edge, Christ is flush with the surface of the canvas. But the lower part of the cross is so recessed that nine people are shown between it and the surface of the picture. It is impossible to tell where the socket is that holds the cross—whether it is on the platform that comes toward us with a wedge shape, or on the earth in front of the platform. The mysterious figure in black who stands and looks straight into the mystery is one of the Sybils who prophesied Christ's fate. Mary is being attended by John, the Magdalene, Mary the wife of Clopas, three of the grieving women Jesus warned of the future, and Joseph from Arimathea, who will bury Jesus.

This is the most theologically rich representation of what the cross means in all of art. It involves prophecy, fulfillment, and promise in a setting that merges time and eternity. Everything revolves around this central fact and mystery of the death of God. The defeat is a triumph—as in the line of a Chesterton poem: "Yet by God's death the stars shall stand."

v. The Glorious Mysteries

BEFORE THE POPE added the luminous cycle to the rosary, those who said it in accord with liturgical seasons prayed the glorious mysteries more than any others—through the whole Ordinary Time from Easter to Advent. There was a certain appropriateness to this, since we members of the mystical body of Christ live in his glorified body, and the Resurrection is the central and ongoing essence of Christianity. But the long season for reciting these mysteries did give a certain imbalance to our contemplation of the gospels, one now remedied.

1. RESURRECTION

We look toward his Son's appearance from the heavens, the one he raised from the dead, Jesus our rescuer from the impending wrath.

(1 Thessalonians 1.10)

[I am] an emissary from Jesus Christ, and from God the Father, who raised him from the dead.

(Galatians 1.1)

. . . to experience him and the energy of his resurrection and the oneness with his sufferings, shaping myself to the pattern of his death, to have a share in his resurrection from the dead.

(Philippians 3.10–11)

My main concern was to pass on to you what was passed on to me—that Christ died for our sins, in accord with the sacred writings, that he was buried, that he arose on the third day, in accord with the sacred writings, that he appeared to Cephas, then to the Twelve. After that, he appeared at the same time to more than five hundred of our brothers, many of whom are still with us, though some have died. And after that he appeared to James, then to all the emissaries.

(1 Corinthians 15.3–7)

Knowing that he who raised Jesus, the Lord, will raise us along with him, and bring us to his side.

(2 Corinthians 4.14)

. . . since we believe in the one who raised from the dead Jesus, our Lord, betrayed for our sins and raised to life for our acquittal.

(Romans 4.24–25)

We who were baptized into Christ were baptized into his death. We were buried with him by this baptism into his death, so that, just as Christ rose from the dead in the dazzle of his Father, so we may live a life entirely new.

(Romans 6.4)

SINCE PAUL'S LETTERS are the earliest part of the New Testament, the passages above, in their probable chronological order, are the first proclamation *(kerygma)* we have of the Resurrection. In the gospels, the resurrection itself is never described. No one witnessed it. The first people to testify to the resurrection were the women who found the tomb empty on Easter morning. Critics have claimed that the notion of the Resurrection came first, and the story of the empty tomb was concocted to support it. But Raymond Brown argues that the tomb itself had to come before the *kerygma*.

> How did the preaching that Jesus was victorious over death ever gain credence if his corpse or skeleton lay in a tomb known to all? His enemies would certainly have brought this forward as an objection; yet in all the anti-Resurrection argumentation reflected indirectly in the gospels or in the second-century Christian apologists we never find an affirmation that the body was in the tomb. There are Christian arguments to show that the body was not stolen or confused in a common burial; but the opponents seem to accept the basic fact that the body can no longer be found. Even in the

Jewish legend that a gardener named Judas took the body only to bring it back, there is a recognition that the tomb was empty. Moreover, the Christian memory of Joseph of Arimathea, which can only with great difficulty be explained as a fabrication, would be rather pointless unless the tomb he supplied had special significance.

Brown also points out that people making up a story would not, in those days, have the testimony come from women, who were considered untrustworthy witnesses. In fact, the women were not even trusted by the male disciples when they reported that the tomb was empty. Saint Augustine noted that the first people to proclaim the risen Lord were women, making up for the false statements of Eve that led to the fall of Adam. They announce the risen second Adam.

On the Sabbath they rested, as required, but at the first glimmer of the next day they went to the tomb with the spices they had kept ready. They found the stone rolled away from the tomb. When they entered the tomb, they could not find the body. As they were puzzling this over, suddenly at their side were two men in luminous garments. The women were frightened and hid their faces with a bow, while the men said: "Why look for one alive in the place of the dead? He is not here. He is risen. Remember his words to you while he was still with you in Galilee, how the Son of Man must be given into the hands of sinners, die on the cross, and rise at the third day." They remembered these words, and leaving the tomb they told all this to the Twelve and everyone else. The women were Mary Magdalene, Joanna, and Mary the mother of James—they and other women with them were telling this to the emissaries. But the story seemed absurd, and they would not believe the women. Peter, nonetheless, did get up and run to the tomb. Looking inside, he saw nothing but the cerements, and went away bewildered by the event.

(Luke 23.56–24.12)

The gospels give different accounts of Jesus' risen appearances, but all agree that the women were the first to discover the facts and believe in them. They were from Galilee and had followed Jesus during his public ministry there, then came to Jerusalem with him—his mother is not mentioned in this group because, as the Cana wedding shows, she took no part in the public ministry. Mary Magdalene is always put first in the list of women who reached the tomb. The gospel of John tells of a private appearance to the Magdalene, and she was clearly a very important witness in the Christian community. Peter is always the first of the Twelve to be a witness to the Resurrection (as in Paul's list at 1 Corinthians 15.5). As for the shifting times and places of the other appearances, Raymond Brown notes that Jesus is often not recognized at first by those who see him. There is something different about his appearance, something numinous or elusive. The risen body is a mystery.

The time and place that characterize earthly existence no longer apply to him in his eschatological state; and so we cannot imagine his dwelling someplace on earth for forty days while he is making appearances and before he departs for heaven. From the moment that God raises Jesus up, he is in heaven or with God. If he makes appearances, he appears from heaven.

The risen Jesus continues to appear to us in his members and his people and his creation. A priest I admire says to those gathered at Mass: "I come here to find Jesus, and when I look at you I do." The power of Christ's life and love still walk the earth, if only we learn to recognize it, as the Magdalene had to recognize Christ in the man she had mistaken for a gardener (John 20.15). Chesterton again:

> On the third day the friends of Christ coming at daybreak to the place found the grave empty and the stone rolled away. In varying ways they realized the new wonder; but even they hardly realized that the world had died in the night. What they were looking at was the first day of a new creation, with a new heaven and a new earth; and in a semblance of the gardener God walked again in the garden, in the cool not of the evening but the dawn.

The importance of the Resurrection cannot be too heavily emphasized. Without it, the cross makes no sense, and neither does the entire Incarnation. We cannot ponder often enough or deeply enough Paul's stress on these truths:

> *If it is our proclamation that Christ was raised from the dead, how can some of you say that there is no resurrection from the dead? If there is no resurrection from the dead, how could Christ have been raised? If Christ was not raised, our proclamation is an empty thing, as is your faith, and we are guilty of false testimony about God, since we were God's witnesses that he had raised Christ, which he could not have done if the dead cannot be raised. If in fact the dead are not raised, then Christ was not raised; and if Christ was not raised, your faith is pointless, and you are still in*

sin's thrall. More than that, those who died in Christ have simply perished. If our hopes in Christ were only for this present life, we are the most pitiable of all human beings. But Christ truly was raised, the first harvest of all who died. As death came through one man, so resurrection comes through one man.

(1 Corinthians 15.12–21)

TINTORETTO

Tintoretto paints the irrepressible energy of life breaking the confines of death. The struggle of the angels with the heavy slab and the guards' oblivion are contrasted with the easy lift-off of Christ bearing his victory banner. The lower part of the picture is a place of death, slumber, unavailing weapons and armor. The upper part opens a whole new era rising up above the picture's limits.

2. ASCENSION

After gathering, they asked him: "Is it time now to restore the reign to Israel?" He told them: "It is not for you to know dates or deadlines, which the Father retains in his exclusive control. But you will assume a power of your own when the Spirit comes to you. Then you will testify to me in Jerusalem and all of Judea and Samaria and to the farthest lands." This said, he was lifted up while they looked on, till a cloud hid him from their eyes. And as they were straining to see where he had gone, suddenly two men in white garments stood by them, to say: "Men of Galilee, why do you stand and gaze at the sky? This Jesus, whom you saw taken up into the sky, will arrive in the same way you saw him go into the sky."

(Acts of the Apostles 1.6–11)

IN THE APOSTLES' CREED we aver: "He ascended into heaven and sits at the right hand of the Father." The last phrase is an allusion to the Jewish scriptural text most cited in the New Testament, Psalm 110: "The Lord said to my lord, you shall sit at my right hand." The ascension and reign with the Father complete the plan of redemption. The whole gospel of John is arranged around the symmetry of Jesus' coming from the Father and returning to the Father. The same pattern is implicit as well in the early Christian hymn cited by Saint Paul, so important to all reflection on the Incarnation:

> *He, having the divine nature from the outset,*
> *thinking it no usurpation to be held God's equal,*
> *emptied himself out into the nature of a slave,*
> *becoming like to man.*
> *And in man's shape he lowered himself,*
> *so obedient as to die, by a death on the cross.*
> *For this God has exalted him,*
> *favored his name over all names,*
> *that at the name of Jesus all knees shall bend*
> *above the earth, upon the earth, and below the earth,*

and every tongue shall acknowledge
that Jesus is the Lord Christ, to the glory of God the Father.
(Philippians 2.6–11)

The last lines of the poem are liturgical—the congregation genuflects to acknowledge Jesus sitting at the right hand of the Father.

Another very early proclamation of the Ascension is a Christian hymn quoted in a letter to Timothy:

> *He was made manifest in the flesh,*
> *and vindicated in the Spirit*
> *in the sight of angels.*
> *Preached to the people,*
> *he was believed in through the world,*
> *as raised to heaven.*
>
> (1 Timothy 3.16)

We have already seen that Raymond Brown denies the temporal or spatial aspects of Jesus' risen appearances. Then why does Luke in the Acts of the Apostles set the Ascension precisely forty days after the Resurrection? He had framed the story in a different way in his gospel (24.51). Luke's gospel told the story of Christ's mission on earth. The Acts tell the story of Christ's mission in the church. He wants to mark the division at the outset of the second story with two events—Christ's return to the Father (Ascension) and his sending of the Spirit (Pentecost). These are told in the biblical imagery of ascensions (of Enoch and Elijah), just as the story of Christ's birth was cast in terms of Jewish literature. Luke wants to mark the end of the period when Jesus appeared to the apostolic generation.

After the Spirit is sent, Christ lives in the church, he acts through the church, through us.

The message is spelled out by Luke in the words "Why do you stand here staring at the skies?" Look around you, he means: Jesus now works through his mystical body, whose feats Luke is about to recount. The message of the Ascension is not that Christ is gone from us, but that he acts now in a different way. He went only to send the Spirit, who expresses the Trinity's incorporation of us into the inner councils of God himself.

TINTORETTO

Tintoretto paints the Ascension as a kind of mystical explosion, the angel wings and victory palms slashing the air like shrapnel from the intense energies released from Christ's rise to the Father. The image of crossing into a new era is presented in the rivulet that divides the rest of the onlookers from Luke, who is seeing the mystery in terms of the scripture he both studies and writes.

3. PENTECOST

When the Fiftieth Day arrived, when all were together, there was a sudden boom like that of a vast wind blowing, and it filled the whole house where they were assembled, and what seemed to be tongues of fire appeared, which separated, then settled, one on each of them. And they were filled with the Holy Spirit, so that they began speaking in different languages, as the Spirit gave them the power to speak.

Staying in Jerusalem were pious Jews from every country under heaven. A crowd of them gathered at the noise being made, and they were stunned because each heard the speakers in his own language. They felt awe and wonder as they said: "Wait. These men speaking, don't they all come from Galilee? Then how can we be hearing them in the language of our native land? Parthians and Medes and Elamites, residents of Mesopotamia, Judea and Cappadocia, Pontus and Asia, Phrygia and Pamphilia, Egypt and the districts of Libya near Crete, visitors from Rome (both Jews and proselytes), Cretans and Arabs—we all hear in our separate languages what they tell us about God's great work." They were awed and puzzled as they asked each other, "What can this mean?" And some were scornful, saying, "They are drunk."

But Peter, standing with the eleven, raised his voice and addressed them: "Men, whether Judeans or just staying in Jerusalem, be clear about this, marking my words: These are not drunken men, as you suspect (it is only nine in the morning). They are fulfilling what the prophet Joel said: 'In the last times, I shall pour my Spirit out over all humankind, so your sons and daughters will be prophets, your young men will see visions, your old men will dream dreams.'"

(Acts of the Apostles 2.1–17)

FAR FROM BEING DESPONDENT at the death of Jesus, his followers had a sudden burst of joyful energy, the work of the Spirit that Jesus sent to continue his work. Pentecost (Fiftieth) was the Jewish Feast of Weeks, celebrated fifty days after Passover. The Christians, still observant Jews, were celebrating this feast when an infusion of life came to the quickening body of the church by the Spirit's action. The church, as the whole people of God, derives its authority only from this action of the Spirit within it.

The afflatus that leads a unified church to speak in many tongues, making itself understood across regional and linguistic and cultural barriers, is the opposite of what happened at the Tower of Babel (Genesis 11.1–9). Where the disciples were gathered, differences produced unity. At Babel, a monolithic unity caused unbridgeable differences between human beings. The builders of the tower were proud of their eminence, creating a monstrous structure to challenge the heavens. From speaking one language, they fell into a babble of mutually non-understood noises. The Lord rebuked this false union of sheer human effort and power:

"Come, let us go down there and confuse their speech, so that they will not understand what they say to one another." So the Lord dispersed them from there all over the earth, and they left off building the city. That is why it is called Babel, because the Lord made a babble of the language of all the world; from that place the Lord scattered men all over the face of the earth.

(Genesis 11.7–9)

Babel divides men when they try to impose a single human program. Pentecost unites men across differences. A universal language of love and salvation is attained by the miracle of the Spirit's action in Christians, themselves the articulated separate members of Christ's mystical body.

Those who speak in the Spirit use healing words, caring words, reconciling words. But the Spirit also prompts bold words, liberating words, challenges to power and untruth. The followers of Christ are marked, in the New Testament, by this *parrhēsia*, literally "all-speak" *(pan-rhēsia)*. It can cause mini-Pentecosts of free speech, as at Acts 4.31: "While they were at their prayers, the place of their assembly vibrated, they were filled with the Holy Spirit, and they spoke out God's word audaciously *[meta parrhēsias]*." The epistle to the Hebrews says (4.16): "Let us approach with audacity *[meta parrhēsias]* the throne of grace, to receive mercy and find grace for our every need." Lying, cowardly evasion, or unwillingness to be open with others or ourselves is a sin against the Spirit given to us at Pentecost.

TINTORETTO

So far as I know, Tintoretto never painted a *Pentecost*.

4. ASSUMPTION OF MARY

Will someone ask, In what way are the dead raised, and in what kind of body do they fare? Don't be a fool. Even a seed you sow does not come to life until it dies. And what you sow is not the plant it will become; it is a mere seed—of wheat, perhaps, or of some other grain. God gives it the plant he has decreed, a different plant according to what seed is sown. And all flesh is not the same, but that of humans, or of beasts, or of birds, or of fish. There are, moreover, heavenly bodies and earthly bodies, and the splendor of the heavenly bodies is one thing, the splendor of earthly bodies another. There is one splendor for the sun, another for the moon, and another for the stars—since star differs from star in splendor.

That is how it is with the resurrection of the dead. Sown in disintegration, the body is raised in integrity. Sown in disgrace, it is raised in splendor. Sown in frailty, it is raised in strength. What is sown as a sensate body is raised as a spiritual body. If there is a sensate body, there is also a spiritual body. For it is written: "The first man, Adam, became a living soul." But the last Adam became a life-giving spirit. Yet the spiritual comes not first; rather the sensate is first, and then the spiritual. The first man came from the clay of earth; the second came from heaven. As the first man was of clay, so are the others claylike. And as the last man was from heaven, so are all his fellows heavenly. And as we have borne the likeness of the man of clay, so shall we bear the likeness of the man from heaven.

(1 Corinthians 15.35–49)

THE GOSPELS DO NOT MENTION Mary's assumption into heaven; but the passage from 1 Corinthians is relevant, because the nature of the body that rose was an issue from the start in Mary's case. There was an early belief, one that lasted in certain heresies, that Mary did not die, she just ascended, living, into heaven—as Elijah was said to have done. This may have been prompted by the fact that there are no traditions about any tomb for Mary, or any relics, as for early martyrs. But deathlessness would have given her a privilege that was denied to her son—he did, after all, die. Therefore the death of Mary became accepted early on. In early iconography, Mary is shown dead with Jesus taking her soul into custody, to be carried to heaven. (Her soul was represented, as in much early art, as a miniature image of her.)

But that left her body behind, to decay—and many were offended by the idea that flesh from which Jesus had taken his flesh could be consumed by worms. Thus the idea of an Assumption of her body after death, like that of the Ascension of her son, was affirmed at least as early as the sixth century, when a liturgical feast was established to celebrate that mystery. Later art is full of images of the Assumption, as are devotions like this mystery of the rosary, which existed as early as the thirteenth century. It was only in the twentieth century—midway in it, as a matter of fact (1950)—that Pope Pius XII proclaimed infallibly that her body was assumed into heaven. This was the first and is still the only use of the infallible power since it was defined as belonging to the papacy, in 1870. It adds nothing to the prayer life of Catholics, who have long prayed to Mary as assumed into heaven. The fact that she could be called to heaven at death is hardly surprising since Jesus said to a less noble human, the good thief, "This day, with me, you will be in Paradise."

But pious older commentators said that only the soul of "Dismas," the thief, was taken to heaven, while his body was left behind. A priest told me when I was in high school that heaven certifiably has only four square feet of physical reality, meaning the bodies of Jesus and Mary. But does Paul's letter to Corinth allow us to think of the risen body as physically spatial in a nonphysical heaven? We say in the creed that we believe in "the resurrection of the body." But we are fools, Paul says, if we think we know what the risen body will be. We might as well, not knowing what an oak tree is, think the acorn was the same as what it would become. The body that rises is the one that gave identity to the whole person. Those effects of identity are not equatable with the passing fortunes of the body that did the individuating.

So the old idea that souls will go to heaven or hell and wait to be reunited with bodies at the last judgment—the bodies being recomposed out of their decayed parts—is a primitive belief that is insupportable now. That crude notion led to endless pointless speculation. For instance: Will a man who lost his leg early in life have it restored in heaven? The scholars who speak of a realized eschatology know that judgment is now, just as death and resurrection are now. (Paul describes them in the passage quoted above in the present tense.) It is the spiritual body that goes to heaven.

Thus Mary's assumption is a symbol and sample of what we all hope for who die in Christ. She, our sister, precedes and comforts us through the deathly portal leading to life.

TINTORETTO

This painting is a companion piece to the *Ascension of Jesus*, in the same building, on the same wall. But where Jesus takes off in a whirl of slashing wings and victory palms, looking up as he leads us higher, Mary looks back on the company she is leaving. It is a very communal picture, where she is surrounded as much by her earthly friends as by the circle of putti that act as her living halo. Indeed, the putto in the tomb seems almost as much to hold her back as to boost her departure. Mary is sad to leave behind those who will, nonetheless, follow her. That is the meaning of this event.

5. CORONATION OF MARY

My soul expands toward the Lord,
  my spirit has found joy in God who saves me,
who looked from on high to his low servant,
    that I should be called blessed down the generations,
for Power itself has expanded me,
  according to his name's holiness.

His mercy runs from each to the next generation,
  for those who hold him in awe.
He has flexed his right arm's power,
  and swept off pride's mad dreamers,
he has brought down the lofty from their thrones,
  and lifted up those under them,
filling abundantly whoever hungers,
  sending the rich off destitute.

For he has taken up his servant Israel's cause
  in memory of mercies past,
according to the word he gave our fathers,
  to Abraham and all his large descent.

(Luke 1.46–55)

THE HEAVENLY CORONATION of Mary is not in the gospels. Some have found it suggested in a passage of Revelation (12.1):

And now a great wonder was in heaven—a woman robed with the sun, with the moon beneath her feet, and twelve stars forming a crown around her head.

The multilayered symbolism of Revelation is notoriously hard to read. Some take the woman of this verse to be the Heavenly Jerusalem, some take her as the church, and others think the image refers directly to Mary. All three could be intended. But the passage that treats Mary as a paradoxical "low servant" who is also a conquering queen is the Magnificat, already considered where she sings this hymn, at the Visitation. It bears renewed reflection at this point. Mary will be "called blessed down the generations." Yet she makes it clear that her power is only what God does through her. The point of her hymn is that God "has taken up his servant Israel's cause in memory of mercies past."

Protestants, who adhere to the Bible, have no reason not to "call Mary blessed," since the Magnificat is in the New

Testament. In that sense, the rosary is not an exclusively Catholic devotion. Only gospel mysteries are contemplated, and even the idea of Mary's assumption into heaven is no more nonbiblical than that of the good thief, while the image of Mary as the church in the new Israel is firmly present in Luke's gospel. The rosary should be an ecumenical prayer, binding us to others through the woman who is the mother of Christ, and therefore of his mystical body. The Second Vatican Council taught that all baptized Christians are members of that body, which prays with and through Mary. Her presence by the side of Christ is as true of the world to come as of the nativity in Bethlehem. She has gone ahead of us, with her son.

TINTORETTO

Renaissance paintings of the Virgin had favored types. Two of the earliest were the *Maestà* (Mary on a throne, looking out at us, with the child on her lap) and the *Umiltà* (Mary seated on the ground, looking down at the child on her lap or on the ground near her). In Venice, Giovanni Bellini created a combination of the two, Mary facing us behind a parapet, with the child on the parapet. But what the Venetians especially revered was the *Coronation of Mary*, a design that was always ecclesiastical in intent—Mary symbolizing the church *(ecclesia)*. It was cosmic in its import, in accord with the Mary of Revelation, wearing her crown of stars.

Behind Tintoretto's largest painting, the *Paradiso* in the Doge's Palace, traces of the first great Venetian *Coronation*, a huge fresco by Guariento, were found. Imitations of it are in the Accademia, by Giambono and by others. These paintings show a huge throne, formed by the saints and angels in a pyramiding structure of the church's "living stones" (1 Peter 2.5). At the summit of this high throne fashioned from the members of the body of Christ, Mary is crowned as the representative of all believers.

Tintoretto took this static design and made it dynamic. The saints are seen as a galactic swirl of exalted human beings, living stars to surround Jesus and Mary at the top of the picture. The cosmic energies of the church fill the flying and dancing figures in a starry dance. Tintoretto treats the church less as a structure than as a charged field—almost as if he foresaw the structure of the universe in atomic terms.

Background Reading

For those who want to know more about the historical, biblical, or theological bases of the practice of the rosary, I recommend these starting points.

HISTORY OF THE ROSARY

Anne Winston-Allen, *Stories of the Rose: The Making of the Rosary in the Middle Ages* (Pennsylvania University Press, 1997).

THE CREED

J. N. D. Kelly, *Early Christian Creeds*, third edition (David McKay, 1972).

Jaroslav Pelikan, *Credo: Historical and Theological Guide to Creeds and Confessions of Faith in the Christian Tradition* (Yale University Press, 2003).

THE OUR FATHER

Raymond E. Brown, S.S., "The Pater Noster as an Eschatological Prayer," in *New Testament Essays* (Doubleday/Image, 1968), 275–320.

Joachim Jeremias, *The Lord's Prayer*, translated by John Reumann (Fortress Press, 1964).

Ernst Lohmeyer, *"Our Father": An Introduction to the Lord's Prayer*, translated by John Bowden (Harper & Row, 1965).

THE HAIL MARY

Nicholas Ayo, *The Hail Mary: A Verbal Icon of Mary* (University of Notre Dame Press, 1994).

THE DOXOLOGY

E. J. Gratsch, "Doxology, Liturgical," in *The New Catholic Encyclopedia*, third edition (Thomson Gale, 2003).

THE JOYFUL MYSTERIES

Raymond E. Brown, S.S., *The Birth of the Messiah: A Commentary on the Infancy Narratives of Matthew and Luke* (Doubleday, 1977).
Joseph A. Fitzmyer, S.J., *The Gospel According to Luke* (Doubleday, 1979).

THE LUMINOUS MYSTERIES

Bruce Chilton, "Transfiguration," in *The Anchor Bible Dictionary*, edited by David Noel Freedman et al. (Doubleday, 1992), 6:640–42.
Raymond F. Collins, "Beatitudes," in *The Anchor Bible Dictionary*, edited by David Noel Freedman et al. (Doubleday, 1992), 1:629–31.
Oscar Cullmann, *Baptism in the New Testament*, translated by J. K. S. Reid (SCM Press, 1964).
Joachim Jeremias, *The Eucharistic Words of Jesus*, translated by Norman Perrin (Fortress Press, 1977).
Saint Augustine, Sermon 191 (Cana); Sermon 227 (Last Supper).

THE SORROWFUL MYSTERIES

B. Brown, "Stations of the Cross," in *The New Catholic Encyclopedia*, third edition (Thomson Gale, 2003).
Raymond E. Brown, S.S., *The Death of the Messiah: From Gethsemane to the Grave* (Doubleday, 1994).

THE GLORIOUS MYSTERIES

Rowan Williams, *Resurrection: Interpreting the Easter Gospel* (Darton, Longman & Todd, 2002).

TINTORETTO

Garry Wills, *Venice, Lion City: The Religion of Empire* (Simon & Schuster, 2001).

PAINTINGS BY
JACOPO ROBUSTI TINTORETTO